THE
Ultimate Stencil
BOOK

ALTHEA WILSON

THE
Ultimate Stencil
BOOK

Photography by
MARK JONES

CONRAN OCTOPUS

Thank you to all the people, including my family,
who have helped me through the years since I came
back from Africa – Myra, Mr Dunkley, Mr Holland,
Mr Whitmarsh, Mr Shaddock and June.

First published as *Stencil Genius* in 1990 by
Conran Octopus Limited
37 Shelton Street
London WC2H 9HN

This paperback edition published in 1994 by Conran Octopus Limited

Reprinted 1995

British Library Cataloguing in Publication Data
Wilson, Althea
   The Ultimate Stencil Book
   1. Decorative arts. Stencilling
   I. Title
   745.73

ISBN 1-85029-835-1

Project Editor Cortina Butler
Art Editors Meryl Lloyd, Kit Johnson
Copy Editor Barbara Mellor
Editorial Assistant Denise Bates
Production Sonya Sibbons

Photographs on pages 1, 8 above, 27-31, 48-49, 93, 101,
110, 114 by Henry Wilson

Typeset by Spectrum Typesetting
Printed in Hong Kong

Contents

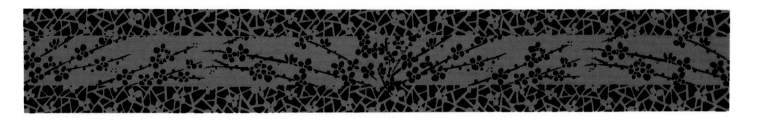

Introduction

The History of Stencilling

Stencilling was really the forerunner to screen printing, using card or paper rather than silk to print out the design. Every ancient civilization seems to have used stencils, from China and Japan to Persia and Europe. Not many of the early examples can be seen today, for as with most of the decorative arts, stencils and stencilling often fell from fashion, to be supplanted by the latest craze. This certainly happened in England, which was always more fashion-conscious than other countries.

Churches and the great halls of the rich made use of the medium from the thirteenth and fourteenth centuries. From the fifteenth century, during the Tudor and Jacobean periods, stencilling was to be seen decorating panelling, ceilings and oak furniture. By the early part of the seventeenth century stencilled wallpaper had taken over from the expensive cloth which until then had been used for covering walls. The paper was not in 10m (33ft) lengths as today, but rather in pieces 1-1.25m (3-4ft) long by 46cm (18in) wide. This was due to the fact that the paper was prepared by hand. A room hung with this hand-stencilled paper has a rather patchwork-like appearance, as no great care was taken in pattern-matching (at least this was the case in the one room I was able to see, some years ago). As with all forms of art, stencilling came and went in popularity: the last few years have seen a revival, which I am sure will wane in time, only to resurface in years to come.

I would venture to say that the Japanese were, in the sixteenth and seventeenth centuries, undoubtedly the masters of the art of stencilling. I thought it might be of interest to look at

Pomegranates in a Bowl

This is one of my favourite designs which unfortunately did not fit in with the new decoration which evolved for the house. Pomegranates in a bowl were framed with plaited ribbon which was then attached to a formal bow, ending in a knotted tassel. The border was influenced by an early Persion textile design. Although this example is printed on paper, it should have been stencilled on to unbleached calico for curtains or blinds.

the history of Japanese stencilling in some detail. The earliest recorded sighting of the use of stencils for decoration was in the Nara period, during the seventh and eighth centuries. Examples of paper from this time show that pigments were sprayed through stencils to print the design. Later, during the eleventh century, leather with stencilled patterns decorated the armour of Samurai warriors. By the end of the sixteenth century, during the Edo period (1615-1868) the stencils had spread into common use, varying in sophistication from the decoration of everyday items used by peasants to the intricate kimonos of the aristocracy.

The methods and techniques of stencilling were closely guarded secrets. The trade of cutting was carried out in the closed communities of Shiroko and Jike on the Ise Peninsula in Mie Prefecture. To this day these are still the main centres of the Japanese stencil business. The paper was hand-made from the inner bark of the paper mulberry tree. The sheets were not large, but did vary in size according to the design to be cut. Three sheets would be sandwiched together using the juice of persimmons, which not only stuck the paper together but also made it waterproof and strong enough to withstand quite hard usage. In the last stages of preparation the stencil paper would be hung in airtight rooms and smoked for several days, presumably rather like our ham or fish. Unlike us, the cutters were so skilled that they were able to stack up several sheets when cutting out the design. Great care would be taken to ensure pattern matching, and more delicate patterns, with large open areas cut away, would be strengthened with a very fine silk mesh placed between two identical cut stencils which were then secured. The paint was then stencilled through the

mesh. This procedure obviated the need for 'legs' or 'bridges'. Their innate gift for translating design from thought into practical application has meant that the Japanese have endowed the world with some of the most beautiful examples of stencilled art and craft.

Parrots amongst Figs

This was designed as a throw for a sofa or chair, to complement hand-printed curtains which had different stencils of parrots and a running border of fig leaves. The figs were stencilled in deep mauve-maroon and the parrots in a combination of all the colours.

Why use Stencils?

Having stated categorically that I hated stencils, I have now done a complete volte-face, as you will see. Once I had started to take the subject seriously I became totally obsessed. At first I cut

At Work in the Kitchen

Most of my designing and stencil cutting is done on the kitchen table (right) so that I can watch TV and cook my supper whilst working. Here I have already tried the leopard on sample paper to make sure that the design is well balanced and cleanly cut, so it is now ready for printing on to cloth. I always find printing the most exciting part because after hours of work you can at last see your idea become a reality.

stencils only in order to ease the repeating of patterns, but slowly I began to realize that 'printing out' stencils gave a more professional look – indeed on cloth it can be difficult to tell if the design has been done by hand or machine. Hence a new world was about to open up. Not always able to afford the machine-printed cloth I liked, I was not happy either to live with what could so easily look home-made. The stencil method solves this problem.

The first stencilling I did was on walls, and it soon became clear to me that if the stencil design was detailed enough, there was really no need to overpaint. Different effects could be achieved by employing either a sponge or a brush. Sponges give a soft and faded look,

Printing on to Water-marbled Paper

The first sample of the fighting tigers (below) has been printed on to grey and black marbled paper. My original intention was to marble the paper then stencil the fighting tigers on to lengths of paper cut to fit the drawing room walls, but this was never done. If you want a similar effect, measure the length of each wall horizontally and, using the heaviest duty lining paper you can buy, cut the paper to size, leaving some extra. Join two widths together using waterproof sticky tape on the back, then roll up the paper ready for water marbling. Lamp-black artist's oil paint, mixed with white spirit, was used for this particular colour. Marble in the usual way (page 20) and leave the paper to dry. Print the sequence of tigers over the marbled paper, rolling up the finished end when the paint is dry. Adjust the spacing of tigers to fit each wall so that you do not have to worry about the pattern matching round corners.

almost dappled, leaving little dots of the background colour to break up the painted area, creating an effect rather like batik. Brushes give a harder, cleaner outline, but can be controlled to leave faded areas if wished.

From walls I progressed to cloth. Here I was to discover that if you just lay down a dark colour – usually black – and leave it to dry, then replace the stencil slightly off register and apply several shades of gold, silver and bronze powders, the dark colour behind throws up the metal paints and creates a shadowed line, giving the design a three-dimensional quality.

With experience I have learnt that printing out can be done on all surfaces. This allows you to build up an entire look, varying the designs from one place or article to another. In one room, for example, I had cut and printed several different kinds of shell and, wishing to carry the theme into the second bathroom, decided that to refresh the original idea I would make the shells 'live' by incorporating octopus and flying fish with crabs and other sea creatures. Although the rooms have a similar feeling they are quite different, not only because I did not use the same stencils, but also because of the different treatment of the walls. In one room the stencils are laid on a background of paper marbled to suggest rippled sand, while the other is lined with a fortunate find of taffeta covering a spectrum of colours from black to pale turquoise. Both rooms clearly remind you of underwater scenes, but in completely opposite moods.

Once I had begun to use stencils they became such a major part of my life that all designs were quickly translated into this cut-out method of application. As you will see there are some almost definite do's and don'ts, although I have taken terrible risks, for instance by leaving out the all-important 'legs' or supports. These hold the whole design together, but also interrupt the flow of the design and are very difficult to paint out. With time and practice, however, you will develop your design ability so that these aids can be avoided.

Creating a Stencil

Researching Design

The world is full of design. Not only does nature provide all one could wish for, but also people have been busy throughout the ages pinching existing patterns and reworking them into new designs. I have never felt guilty about availing myself of any ideas to hand: I came to the conclusion long ago that nothing today is really original, since design has been going on for millions of years. Apart from anything else we all translate ideas in a very personal way and so make them our own.

If you have chosen a historical subject, the best places to start looking for inspiration are the museums, historic houses open to the public and the wealth of books on almost any subject one can think of. Most local libraries carry a plentiful selection of books on the history of art, and are willing to order if you want a specialized subject. Magazines are another source of ideas, as is window-shopping round antique markets and junk shops.

Once you have found the flower or bird that you feel will enhance your design, it is often easier to copy from someone else's painting or drawing, as they will already have done most of the work for you by translating the subject matter into two dimensions and simplifying the lines and colours. Most handy are books of hand-painted illustrations of botanical and natural subjects. Antique crockery can be another marvellous source: we seem to have an abundance of porcelain and china from all over the world, which can be seen not only in the wonderful displays to be found in museums, but also in sale rooms, and of course in shops selling modern manufactured and hand-painted goods.

I have always thought that researching designs is important not only for the

Developing the Design

This design illustrates three kinds of cacti and pineapple in pots. Because the overall theme is rather formal I have used an adaptation of the Chinese fence pattern (page 57), adding the stylized scales from the pineapple skins to solidify the otherwise open design. I had thought that this rather masculine design would be suitable for a small study, either stencilled on to the walls or printed over the blinds and curtains.

sake of accuracy, so that passers-by cannot question the content of your work, but also for its own intrinsic interest and for the sense of confidence and authority that it gives you. It also often leads you on to new, previously unthought-of areas, sparking your imagination off into thinking of ideas which might be quite contrary to your first notions.

Developing a Design for Stencilling

Having chosen what sort of subject matter you want to use for stencilling on either walls or cloth you will need to simplify the idea in order to achieve the best result. The method of cutting holes in card or paper and pushing the paint through does not produce the sort of delicate images that are possible with hand-painting. The finished effect is more of a design than a picture, so this must always be at the back of your mind when you are searching for ideas.

The next thing to consider is that the cut-out must be self-supporting. At first I used 'legs' or 'bridges': thin strips of paper left at strategic points of the design, especially where you have vast open areas with nothing to hold them in place. This method has its drawbacks, because after you have finished stencilling you need to go round and touch in these unpainted strips. I found that however careful I was not to overlap the paint on to the stencilled area, the touched-in part still showed and for me spoiled the finished effect. This led me to try and fit my design to the method I was using. I realized that it is important when designing to calculate your spaces, always making sure that the larger cut-out areas are supported. If you are cutting out a clump of tall thin reeds, for

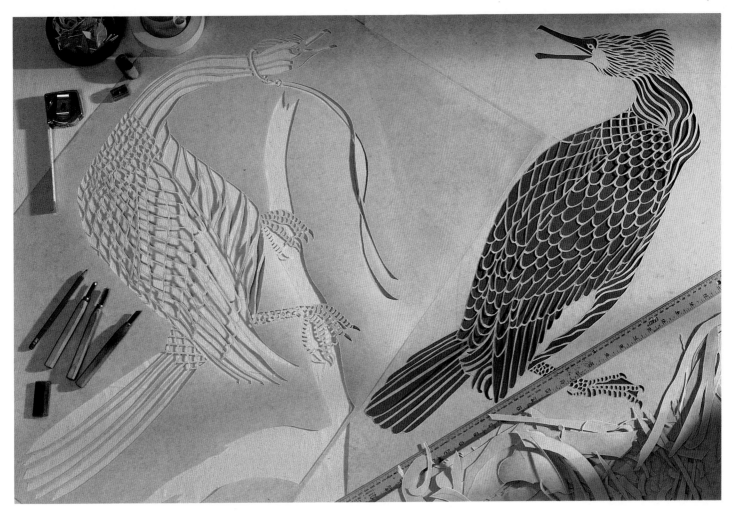

example, where the very nature of the plant requires long thin lines, either add equally spaced notches down the stem to suggest bamboo-like segments, or arrange your design so that a couple of the reeds have been bent over in the wind, letting them lean over the upright spikes. This will tie the straight cuts together, giving them extra strength and holding them in place so that they do not become distorted while you are stencilling.

Assembling your Equipment

The tools and equipment needed for stencilling are not only quite cheap, but also relatively few. You should be able to find all you need at your local art shop. First and foremost is a good-

Choosing your Equipment

Not much equipment is required for cutting stencils. Instead of using a scalpel I work with Japanese wood-carving knives because they are more comfortable to hold over long periods of time. The birds I have just finished cutting here are cormorants: these birds were trained by the Chinese to catch and bring back fish, which is why the left-hand bird has a ring round his neck to prevent him from swallowing them.

quality cutting knife with a proper handle: I find that a scalpel is too flimsy for prolonged cutting and I prefer to use knives with wooden handles as they help to prevent blisters. I now use Japanese wood-carving and linoleum-cutting knives, which come with their own whetstone so that you can keep the blades constantly razor sharp – essential in order to achieve clean cuts. Whetstones are quite simple to use: you spread a tiny amount of oil on the stone, to prevent the metal blade from overheating and distorting, and with an even pressure massage the bevelled edge of the blade up and down on it, moving the blade in figures of eight to prevent the stone from wearing down unevenly and getting a dip in the middle. If on the other hand you have a knife which has changeable blades, make sure to keep plenty in stock so that you can fit new ones whenever required.

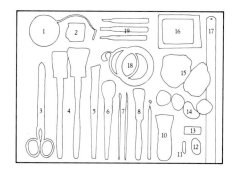

EQUIPMENT
stencilling tools

1 Measuring tape

2 Steel tape

3 Wallpaper scissors

4 Long-handled stencil brush

5 Fitch

6 Squirrel mop

7 Pencil brushes

8 Decorator's brush

9 Pencil

10 Stencil brush

11 Chalk

12 Rubber (eraser)

13 Whetstone

14 Face sponges

15 Potter's sponges

16 Car sponges

17 Metal ruler

18 Masking tape

19 Japanese wood-carving knives

The best stencil paper comes in two sizes: 89cm × 61cm (36in × 24in), which is yellow, and 76cm × 50cm (30in × 20in), which is brown/buff. This tough, waterproof paper, which is actually more like card, is produced by soaking manila paper in linseed oil. It can be made at home, but it is much easier and quicker to buy, leaving you more time to concentrate on the end result. A cutting mat, while not essential, is very useful, especially if you wish to cut stencils on a regular basis. Otherwise, you can use offcuts of lino, though they wear out more quickly.

Next I always have a selection of natural face sponges and the ones that potters use for smoothing clay, which have very small holes and can be bought either in art shops or in specialized pottery equipment suppliers. The brushes I prefer to use are the long-handled French ones, which come in two or three sizes. The normal short-handled brushes can be just as effective, but I find that after a very few minutes I get hand cramps. In fact if you intend to do only a restricted amount of stencilling, you can use a 2.5cm (1in) decorator's brush, especially if the hairs are worn with age. You will also need odd bits and pieces of equipment such as masking tape for repairs and joining paper together.

Lastly the paint: I normally use household emulsion and sometimes, if I cannot find the colour I want in emulsion, gouache. Gouache is not fast, so you cannot wash cloth that has been stencilled with it, and if you wish to sponge down a wall the surface must be sealed. Gold powders, which seem to play a large part in my designs, can be found in art shops. All receptacles for holding paint and powders are taken from the kitchen cupboard.

Drawing the Design

For your first stencil I suggest you choose a simple subject such as a bold butterfly or flower. Until you get used to cutting it is better to draw up the design in charcoal or pencil, then felt-tip pen.

Drawing the Design
These grasshoppers were drawn up in pencil then outlined in black felt-tip pen for clarity.

EQUIPMENT
for drawing and cutting stencils
Stencil paper
Pencil, chalk or charcoal
Steel ruler and rubber (eraser)
Tracing paper
Pins and masking tape
Cutting tools
Cutting mat

Charcoal and felt-tip are both a bit messy, getting all over your hands, but they give a thick line, so that if you need to cut away the paper on both sides of the line all you have to do is follow the outside edges of the charcoal line, leaving strands of paper which are all of equal width dividing the open spaces. If you cannot draw, you can simply photocopy the butterfly, enlarging it to the required size, and then either reverse trace it on to the paper or use the traditional embroiderer's method: prick with a pin along the lines, keeping the holes quite close together, then lay the drawing on to the stencil paper and rub powdered charcoal through the holes. Lift the paper and blow off the excess powder, then draw round your pattern with charcoal or pen. The more advanced you become, the easier you will find it to use a soft pencil which glides over the oiled surface. There is also the grid system: draw measured squares over the picture or on to tracing paper which can be laid over your example. Rule correspondingly larger squares on the stencil paper, and copy into each of the larger squares the exact contents of each of the smaller squares. This method should enable you to make a very close copy of your original.

In order not to risk sponging or painting over the edges of the stencil when you are working, it is advisable to leave approximately 5cm (2in) round each drawing. If you do overlap, as I often have, it really does not present much of a problem. Before cutting the design out, simply go round any area of the paper which does not have a thick enough border attaching masking tape to the back and front, so doubling the width of the edge.

If you want to achieve a repeat pattern on a border, the simplest way, if it is made up of only one or two motifs, is to cut out the complete repeat, then work out the spaces to be left between each part of the design. Using your cut-out stencil, print the pattern on to the paper and cut it out. This not only means that the motif is exactly repeated but saves time trying to draw the design accurately several times. When drawing up a large design that must continue in a repeat pattern, I always leave a border of about 2.5 cm (1 in) on the left-hand side, so that as I cut the stencil I can adjust the drawing to follow exactly from one end to the other. This will be fully explained in the cutting procedure (below). If the design requires several sheets of stencil paper, ultimately to be joined together, I normally join the sheets temporarily and draw my whole design and then take them apart again so that during the cutting I can work on one sheet at a time. Leave a 7.5 cm (3 in) space on the edges to be joined. I repeat this on all the sheets, then join them one by one with masking tape on both sides and the cutting is completed. The longest stencil I have ever worked with is probably just over two sheets: any more and I find the whole piece becomes unmanageable.

Cutting the Stencil

The first thing I do after I have assembled all my equipment is to 'plaster up', winding masking tape round all the points of pressure where I am most likely to get blisters (I find it doesn't help much after they have already started to appear). If you have to wrap the tape round your hand to protect the joint at the base of your first finger, hold your hand stretched open while you are doing so, otherwise it restricts your movements. The only other way of avoiding blisters is to rub methylated spirits into your hands regularly for a few weeks until the skin becomes hardened, but you end up with hands like a navvy.

When I want to start cutting stencils I always clear everything off the table except for the tools I need for the job. This leaves me free to swivel the paper in any direction, so that I do not have to stretch or cut in an uncomfortable position. Normally the cutting starts near the centre of the design so that maximum strength is retained while you work. It is advisable to cut small delicate areas of the design before cutting larger portions. Holding the knife in a comfortable position, simulate a draw-

Cutting the Stencil

Start with the small sections – when you remove the larger portions it weakens the finer parts of the design.

Tidying the Edges

Sometimes tufts of paper get left behind: it is important to clean these up before using the stencil.

ing motion. I have read that you do not need to apply great pressure, but have found that in order to cut a clean straight line there is no other way. Otherwise you will find that when you lift out the rejected pieces of paper, dog-ears will be left in awkward places, and needless to say these all have to be cut or else they will spoil your design.

Make the first incision with the point of the knife, then level it out to use the whole blade, coming up on to the point again towards the end of the cut. I usually cut towards myself, except for long, straight lines when you cut away from yourself (this takes more practice). If your knife slips it is not the end of the world, for stencils can easily be repaired. Place a portion of masking tape on both sides of the paper then simply recut. This method is also used to repair the more delicate areas which invariably break with constant use. If your design includes fine lines, you will need to cut out thicker lines than you would draw, otherwise the paint will not be able to leave its mark.

Almost every border has a repeat. To ensure that you have an exact match so that the join does not show when you move the stencil along, leave at least 7.5 cm (3 in) uncut at one end of the design, loop the paper into a circle, overlap the cut end on to the uncut end and secure it temporarily with masking tape. Then with a pencil, mark the join-up points through the spaces cut in the design. Lay the stencil flat and finish cutting. I have found it helps to rule lines round the perimeter of the design, and even make notches on the edge of the sheet to help with lining up and joining. Although I have never felt the need for them, you can also make corners to match up with the border, leaving them unattached so that they can be used as and when.

Now that the cut stencil is complete I suggest you try it out on rough paper: when you see the design printed out you will be able to correct any faults and alter parts that need rebalancing. Because paper is expensive I have taken to using ordinary lining paper, which costs very little.

Using the Stencil

Choosing Paints

Normally I use household emulsion paints because they are made with a high content of acrylic and so are waterproof once dry, easy to handle when trying to keep your equipment clean, and can be mixed with gouache or powder paint, which it stabilizes. Oil-based paint has several disadvantages for me: it is shiny (except for under-coat), leaving hard lines which catch the light, it gives off fumes, and all the white spirit or solvents needed to clean your brushes and sponges can act as an irritant if you are working with them constantly. Oil-based paint also costs considerably more.

I have taken to using emulsion not only on walls but also on cloth. Having tried using dyes in paint form, I found it harder to achieve the density of colour I wanted, and I also discovered that, depending on the cloth, colour bleeding was a greater risk. To cap it all, you have to iron wherever you have applied the dye in order to fix the colour.

Applying Paint Through the Stencil

Whether you choose to use a sponge or a brush the paint must always be mixed to the consistency of thick custard. Put a quantity of your mixture on a plate to one side, leaving room on the plate to tap off any excess. When stencilling on to walls I take the usual precautions by laying down dust sheets, then gather together all my equipment and lay it out on a small table. If the stencil is too large to hold by hand I secure it with masking tape, an idea I am not very keen on, however, as the wall finish underneath can all tee easily lift off with the tape when the stencil is removed.

EQUIPMENT
for applying the paint
Cut stencils
Emulsion, gouache and powder paint
French stencil brush and fitch
2.5 cm (1 in) decorator's brush
Natural face sponge or potter's sponge
Car sponge
Masking tape
Selection of mixing bowls and plates
Dust sheets and clean rags
Bucket and clean water
Newspaper or lining paper

Applying and Choosing Paints

Because this stencil (above) is small I have not taped it to the cloth, but it must be held firmly. I keep gold powder in preserving jars (opposite) which should always be kept closed otherwise the powder flies everywhere.

Having applied paint to the face of your sponge or dipped the brush, get rid of any excess by tapping on to the clean side of the plate or a piece of newspaper, then pounce the paint over the cut-out areas of the stencil, making sure that each corner receives its fair share. It is up to you whether you apply the paint evenly or let it fade in places. When you have covered the whole area lift off the stencil, being careful that it doesn't flap back on to the wall. If you are going to use it again immediately check that no paint has seeped on to the back. If it has, gently drag the stencil over a clean, lint-free cloth to remove the paint and check again: if it is still wet you will have to wait until the paint has dried, otherwise carry on until you are finished. Sometimes, if the job is massive, I cut two stencils so that I can rest one, leaving it to dry while I continue the job with the second one.

The correct method of going round corners is to 'hinge' the stencil by cutting it in half vertically, then rejoining it with masking tape on both sides. This allows the stencil complete manoeuvrability round corners, whether convex or concave. My first reason for not practising what I preach is that in my house nothing is square and there are all sorts of architectural peculiarities so that in no time the stencils would be in shreds. The other reason is laziness. I have overcome the problem by creasing the paper into place or just pushing it into the corner and then painting one side at a time. It works. If you have not cut another stencil and feel the one you are using is becoming rather clogged with paint and may not finish the room, I suggest you just stencil the design on to another piece of stencil paper, ready to cut out as and when the need arises.

Do not let your brushes or sponges dry out or they will be ruined. It is of the

Over-painting

This Chinese peony is a good example of over-painting. First I stencilled the flower on to blue-dyed cloth in black emulsion, and when it was dry I replaced the stencil slightly off register to leave a shadow. Then I applied the silver powders lightly, allowing the metallic paint to fade so leaving the black to show through in the body of the flower as well as round the edges.

utmost importance to keep your equipment in tip-top condition. If you are using several different colours and thus need to lay aside your brush, wrap it in a damp cloth. If you put it in to soak, however carefully you squeeze the water out there always seems to be plenty left in the ferrule which dribbles all down your arms or – worst of all – suddenly gulps on to the stencil. Put your sponge in to soak, when you have finished with it, squeeze out the excess water when you want to reuse it, then to make sure it is dry enough wrap it in a tea towel and press again. Alternatively keep several sponges so that you always have a clean one handy. After a day's painting I always clean everything, leaving it to dry overnight, so that I am ready to start off in the morning with clean dry tools.

Being of a lazy turn of mind I usually do not cut out a different stencil for each colour. I know you are supposed to, but quite frankly I want to get on with the job, so for the most part I have found a way round this dilemma. To stencil an amaryllis lily with red flowers and green leaves I start off with the leaves and stem in green, and when I am too close to the flower for comfort I block it out with a piece of paper. When it is time to apply the red I lift off the piece of paper blocking out the flower and use a new sheet of paper to block out the green areas so as not to smudge the paint left on the first piece of paper on to the cloth or wall. If you have cut the flower too close to the leaf, and cannot block one out without overlapping the other, use a pencil brush or fitch to dab gently through the stencil until the paint has built up to the correct density.

If you should by any chance make a mistake or have a run of paint, don't panic. Leave the area to dry, then simply paint out the patch with the background colour and proceed with your stencil when the surface is ready. Small smudges and dabs of paint from the stencil can be touched in and rough edges straightened if need be when the whole job is finished.

Over-painting

Over-painting can be used to achieve two different effects. First you can add more detail by either shading or outlining your subject. Usually I choose a fine pencil brush and hand-paint any additions requiring a more delicate touch, such as feathers, eyes or veining on leaves. You can also use over-painting to create a three-dimensional effect: stencil the first coat on to your wall or cloth, preferably in a dark colour, and leave it to dry thoroughly. Mix the second colour and reapply the stencil, moving it slightly so that when the second coat of paint is applied to one side, instead of matching it up exactly with the first image the first coat will register a line or shadow. Then pounce the paint on lightly, leaving the undercoat to show through.

I do most of my over-painting with gold powders. Mixing these is not difficult: spoon the amount you think you will need into a pudding basin (an old one kept for the purpose, as you cannot wash the mixture off). Put a small amount of button polish to one side of the basin and draw in a little of the gold powder. Taking your stencil brush, mix them to form a gold paste (not too thick), and apply it quickly. Do not mix all your gold powders at once, as the button polish dries very rapidly and you will be left with a lump of gold which cannot be re-used. When you have finished, wash your brush immediately in methylated spirits before the polish hardens. If you intend to use large amounts of gold powders you can store the brush in the button polish *ad infinitum*, as long as the jar is kept airtight. I do not use sponges with gold powders as they tend to go hard when immersed in methylated spirits.

EQUIPMENT
for over-painting stencils

Cut stencils
Emulsion, gouache and powder paint
Mixing bowls and plates
Gold powders
Button polish, brush and mixing bowl
Methylated spirits
Cloth
Natural face sponge or potter's sponge
French stencil brush, fitch and fine pencil brush

Combining Stencils and Backgrounds

Assembled in this picture are several examples of stencils used on different surfaces. The shells in the foreground have been printed on to water-marbled paper. Each of the shells is an individual stencil, which gives the freedom to place them at random. The tiled dado shows how stencils can be used to form a repeat pattern which would take hours to hand-paint. Here the tiles were stencilled in blue and then over-painted in blue/black to add detail and to outline the acanthus leaves. The birds are done using the same method, but have not been antiqued. The peony design is also made up of separate stencils so that the design is not obviously repeated.

Combining Stencils

It goes without saying that a smaller stencil is easier to control than a massive sheet of paper. If I have a design such as the African animals (page 62), made up of several different sizes and shapes, I usually cut all the subjects separately. In that case it required some 38 symbols to complete the total. Many of my designs are constructed in this manner, as I find it gives me the freedom to interchange the patterns, thereby achieving a collection in which each element is slightly different.

Another reason why I like assembling stencils to make up a whole is because they can be placed at random over the surface – whether directly on to a wall or on to paper or cloth. I feel that if you are hand-printing cloth or paper you do not necessarily have to adhere to the pattern repeat formula that manufacturers are bound by. In fact I would rather be able to see that the cloth has no pattern repeat, then you know that it has been specially printed for you. Part of the reason for doing the printing yourself, of course, is to acquire a finished design which is completely original without looking at all home-made.

Special Effects

Fantasy Malachite on Paper

The method explained here is quick, easy and most suitable for covering large areas of paper with a malachite stone finish, rather than the more detailed gem-quality finish which is better for small areas.

First of all put a dust sheet over a large table. Lay out the cut length of paper and secure the ends with masking tape. Paint the emerald green emulsion on to the clean dry paper, leave it to dry and then apply a second coat. While you wait for this to dry, prepare the graining tools used to form the striation patterns found in natural stone.

Take a flat 3.5-4cm (1½-2in) square flat rubber (eraser) and cut off one corner with a scalpel. Do the same to the adjacent corner, making a smaller cut. This will give you two widths of stripe. Cut teeth of various widths out of the uncut bottom edge. For a different, finer finish, I use modified rubber combs: cut off some of the teeth to form another tooth pattern; in places I leave wide gaps.

When the emerald green paint is totally dry, apply two or more coats of button polish or polyurethane varnish to the paper if needed. Button polish dries very quickly.

With your decorator's brush and dark green, paint over the varnished paper covering an area 30cm (1ft) square. Place the blunt end of an oblong rubber on to the wet paint and twist it clockwise to form a close group of circles. Draw fine lines around each circle with a pencil rubber, then, working quickly round the group with the cut rubber or comb, lift off the paint creating swirls and zigzags by using the different implements alternatively. Before the paint dries, very gently pass a

A Dado in Malachite

Although the formal Empire stencil on this dado appears black it is printed in the same green as the malachite.

EQUIPMENT
for fantasy malachite

Emerald emulsion paint
(made by mixing viridian green and chrome yellow powders and a little black emulsion to a true emerald and then adding this to white emulsion)
Dark black/green emulsion paint
(made by adding viridian green and a touch of chrome yellow powders to black emulsion paint)
Two 5cm or 10cm (2in or 4in) decorator's brushes
Heavy lining paper
Button polish or polyurethane varnish
Squirrel mop for applying varnish
Selection of rubbers (erasers), rubber-toothed combs, rubber date stamp
Goose feather
Masking tape

---

dry goose feather horizontally over the vertical lines, wiggling the feather slightly as it drags the paint.

Work as quickly as possible and do not allow the edges of the square to dry out because you must continue to add dark green paint and join up the pattern lines until the whole sheet of paper is covered. It is also essential not to let your combs, rubbers and goose feather become clogged with paint. I usually keep a damp cloth near at hand so that I can wipe off the excess. Use a saucepan of water to wash the feather, then wipe it dry on a clean cloth.

Finally, once the malachite paper has completely dried and been hung on the wall, several coats of button polish or polyurethane varnish can be applied to give a high sheen, similar to polished stone. This can sometimes look overpowering though, and I suggest that you practise on sample sheets.

Over-printing on Water-marbled Paper

To give stencilled designs a more sophisticated effect, I decided to print on to water-marbled papers. Once the paper has dried, the stencilling process is exactly the same as before, except that any mistakes cannot be corrected. To put it bluntly, you've had it.

Preparing the marbled surface is quite easy, but I suggest you have a practice run. It is easiest to start off with shorter lengths of paper. Use the heaviest grade of lining paper you can buy. Measure the drop from ceiling to skirting board, leaving about 15cm (6in) just in case. Then work out how many drops you need. Measure and cut the paper to length, rolling up each drop.

Mix artist's oil paint to a watery consistency with turpentine or white spirit. Fill the bath three-quarters full. Assemble all the paper and paint within easy reach, along with a plastic bucket and a large cardboard box. Give the paint mixture a good stir, then pour some into the water. With the brush swish the paint through the water to disperse it, then leave it to rise to the surface. Lift the length of paper over the bath with one hand holding the rolled part away from you and the other holding the free end nearest to you. Stretch it out to the width of the bath keeping the rolled part uppermost and away from the water. Let the paper float on top of the water, so that the paint soaks into the dry paper. Lift and roll up the end nearest to you, letting the other side unroll to the width of the bath. Lay the next section of paper on to the surface of the water, trying not to leave an unpainted area between the finished part and the new starting point. Carry on till the whole roll has been processed. More paint can be added between lifts.

Once you have accustomed yourself to this water marbling you will be able to start experimenting with the different effects you can achieve by moving the paper from side to side as it lies on the water. Do not worry if it sinks: it just means the paint will cover both sides. Try not to twist or ruckle the wet paper as it will tear very easily. Place the first roll into a bucket to drain, then transfer it to a cardboard box. When the box is full carry the paper to a place where it can be hung out to dry. If you have nowhere convenient spread a dust sheet on the floor and lay the paper flat.

You will notice that the first section of marbling will be darker than the last: you can even out the colour by using less paint in the beginning, then adding small amounts during the process. If you want to use more than one colour you can do so in two ways. The first is to introduce the second colour into the water after the other has risen, trying not to over-swish the paint. The second method is to use one colour and then let the paper dry completely because the paint cannot be absorbed by wet paper. You can then start all over again with another mix.

Material Differences

The fighting tigers and other co-ordinating prints are stencilled on to water-marbled paper and natural calico.

EQUIPMENT
for water-marbling paper

Artist's or student's oil paint
Turpentine or white spirit
Heavy lining paper
Fitch
Mixing bowls
Bucket and large cardboard box
Dust sheet

EQUIPMENT
for antiquing

Sandpaper, rough and smooth
Emulsion paint
Mixing bowls
10cm (4in) decorator's brush
Car sponge
Rags, bucket and clean water

Antiquing

Antiquing is done when all the stencilling is finished and thoroughly dry. The easiest but messiest method is to sandpaper the wall. Choose the grade of sandpaper according to the desired result: the smoother the sandpaper the more delicate the end finish. Sand off the whole area evenly, taking care to apply less pressure around the seams of lining paper and any bumps in the plasterwork. The finished effect softens the definition of the design, leaving a mellowed room which might have been painted a century earlier.

The other method uses an extremely watery paint solution mixed to the colour of dirty dishwater. Apply the mixture with a brush or dip the face of a clean damp car sponge into the paint. Work quickly over the entire area pushing the watery colour around as evenly as you can. Try not to let the edges of the paint dry out or you will end up with watermarks and lines. If you do not care for the blotchy finish you can easily remedy it once it has dried by sanding off as above. Depending on the result you want you can use either method or both and in any order.

Different Surfaces

Wood, Stone and Tiles

For stencilling on to wood and stone use the same methods already described with emulsion paint. Wood may be sealed with button polish for extra protection: this is applied with a mop brush made from squirrel, the fine hairs ensuring the smoother application of liquid polish and leaving no tell-tale lines. Normally, however, ordinary bees-wax polish will serve the purpose perfectly well, and this polish has the added advantage that it feeds the wood at the same time.

Tiles are a different matter. They need refiring to fix the new design. I have found through the years that some tiles stand up to refiring better than others. I believe moisture levels play a significant part in this: once the tile has left the factory it tends to gather moisture, thus the older the tile the

---

EQUIPMENT
for stencilling wood, stone and tiles

Emulsion paint
Button polish or coach varnish
Methylated or white spirit
Bees-wax polish
White tiles
Onglaze colours
Tile racks
Mixing dishes
Natural sponge with large holes
Selection of brushes
Clean 5 cm (2 in) decorator's brush
Water in a mug

One Design used in Different Ways

I liked the pots and Adire cloth that feature in one of my paintings so much that I decided to repeat the picture on some tiles which I intended to use in my kitchen.

---

more likely it is to break. The basic technique for stencilling is as previously described, but instead of paint you need to use a water-based onglaze, available from specialist pottery suppliers. It comes in small tubes, rather like watercolour paint, and is of about the same consistency. It is also possible to buy oil-based colours, but I have never done so and would not therefore be able to advise on their use.

Make sure your tile is not cracked, by holding it up to the light and looking across the glazed surface. If as you are working you notice a line appearing which will not go away even if you wipe the glaze off and reapply it, then throw the tile out because it will split in the kiln and in doing so may damage other tiles or even the elements.

An antiqued effect can be achieved by mixing a dirty dishwater-coloured onglaze, and then sponging over your design with a natural large-holed sponge, using dabbing movements to create a dappled effect which also smudges the stencil slightly, softening the harder lines. Alternatively you can let the onglaze dry, then with a 5 cm (2 in) dry decorator's brush lightly brush over the top of the design using a fanning movement and only just touching the surface. This will wear off the onglaze, giving the tile the appearance of great age. I suggest you practise before attacking the real thing as it is an extremely delicate task: if you are too heavy-handed the whole design will simply disappear.

When you pick up the tiles to place them in the tile racks take care to touch only the very edges. The onglaze is not stable until it has been fired at about 790°C (1454°F), at which temperature it melts and fuses permanently with the factory finish. For firing instructions turn to your kiln manual or enquire at a specialist pottery supply shop.

Doors and Radiators

In my opinion doors are a natural progression from dados: if you have painted or stencilled your dado in a different design from the main part of the room then you should also include the door. It is not always necessary to cut a design to fit the panels: often with a bit of juggling some part of the overall pattern can be made to fit.

Radiators are another matter. Sometimes I wish I had never started the idea of painting or stencilling them to match the dado. Wherever I have done this everyone neverendingly remarks on the fact, which I find irritating, as the intention is to make them disappear, not to draw attention to them. One time I conducted a little experiment in the kitchen, leaving the radiators totally undecorated. Of course nobody noticed or said a word: perhaps we are so used to seeing these ugly necessities that the eye glides over them as if they do not exist – which is why, after you have struggled for hours to overcome the difficulties of painting them to match the background, it is annoying when everyone rushes in the room only to remark on this one feature.

The only advice I can give on the stencilling of radiators is to start when you are fresh, not at the end of a hard day. You will find that you just have to manage somehow to bend the stencil over the corrugated surface, using sponges, fitches – in fact anything that will produce the effect you want. Often I have been reduced to hand-painting large areas where the stencil simply would not lie flat enough, as for example in the large bathroom (page 52).

Stencilling on Cloth

Now that I have discovered the miracles that are possible when you print cloth yourself, I shall probably no longer be the world's most extravagant purchaser of printed chintzes and linens. It is possible to use stencils cut for any other

The Perils of Radiators

When I designed the dado for my bathroom (page 53) I had forgotten all about this radiator – the worst one I ever had to stencil. Much of it had to be hand-painted.

EQUIPMENT
for stencilling cloth

Cut stencils
Emulsion, gouache and powder paint
Gold powders
Button polish and mixing bowl
Methylated spirits
Masking tape
Scissors
Measuring tape
Natural sponges
Cloth of your choice
Calico
Fabric dye
Spray starch
Scalpel

purpose on nearly all weaves. Most cloth can be printed, including panne and ordinary velvets, duchesse satin, taffetas, net piqué, damask, wild silk and heavy winter cloth, melton and felts. Crêpe is not receptive: at first it appears fine, then when the paint or gold powders dry the cloth begins to shrink, leaving the unprinted areas wrinkled and the printed areas rock hard.

The most versatile cloth is calico. Not only is it cheap, thus allowing you to indulge in enormous quantities, but it can also be left *au naturel* or dyed to almost any colour. The simplest way to do this is in the washing machine: depending on the amount of dye you use the colour can vary from lighter tones to deep rich shades. Do allow for shrinkage, as you have to set the machine on the hottest wash: as far as I can remember, in every 2.75m (9ft) drop the cloth will lose about 10cm (4in). When the material is nearly dry, out comes the iron on the hottest thermostat reading: if the cloth has dried out too much, spray it either with water from a fine garden spray or with starch. Now you are ready to begin stencilling.

I lay all cloth out on a flat surface with a smooth dust sheet underneath, holding it in position by attaching masking tape at intervals down the sides. Put your stencil in place, again using masking tape to secure it, then carry on in the normal way. When you have finished the length on the table pull the material down and lay the painted part on the floor, keeping it flat until it dries, and start on the next length. When painting any cloth you need to make sure your mix is fairly thick, or else bleeding will occur. If you drop a small blob of paint on to the cloth by mistake it is sometimes best to leave it to dry, then very cautiously scrape it off with a razor blade or scalpel. I have found that wiping paint off simply leaves a larger watery stain.

For paint I use emulsion and gold powders. Be careful if you use gouache or powder paints as these are not waterproof and so the finished material cannot be washed. I cannot recommend dry cleaning them, either, as I have not tried it. I have also used dye in paint form, which is quite expensive and not as dense as I normally require, but as I was printing pillow cases and a duvet cover – which have to be washed innumerable times – I thought I would play safe. On the cotton duvet cover there was no problem, but on the pillow slips, which were a cotton and polyester mix, the dye bled no matter how careful I was. After several washes on the correct machine programme it also faded considerably, even though I had ironed the coloured area as instructed. I was not impressed.

REPEAT PATTERNS

As I have already mentioned, I do not always adhere to pattern repeats. When I want the design to flow over the material evenly in a repeat pattern I do one of two things. Having chosen the cloth you want to use, measure up the width and simply cut your stencil to fit across it. Cut the sides of the stencil to repeat, and leave the top and bottom to match up as you move the stencil (as long as the design is not vertical). If you have the energy and the pattern requires it you can cut all four sides to repeat. My way of overcoming all this hard work is not to allow the design to touch the edges, which means that you can sail along, moving the stencil down the cloth with no matching up worries.

If a design is made up of separate stencils I simply guess the spacing – after a time I discovered that I was accurate to within a couple of centimetres (less than an inch). If you are making curtains the pattern can carry on down the whole length without a repeat, only doing so on its partner. Sometimes it is fun to place the different stencils at random, and just make sure that no two similar symbols end up next to each other.

CLOTHES

Stencilling on to clothes seemed a natural progression after stencilling on to cloth and it is fun. I find the easiest

The Tiger Coat

I printed the tiger in black emulsion (top) before the coat was sewn together so that I could match up his body which carries over on to the front of the coat. Because the stencil was not cut for this specific job I had great difficulty in fitting the tiger to his best advantage. I made the coat reversible (above), because it saved time since you do not have to line it, and because you can wear whichever side takes your fancy. The stylized carnations are stencilled in black emulsion.

Curtains and Swags

My stairwell has always presented problems over which design or colour to use on the curtains. Because you can see them from the drawing room – half a floor down – I decided this time to combine the cherry blossom and twig design from my kitchen (page 57) with Chinese vases and flowers from the bedroom (page 40), stencilling the entire design in the blue paint used in the drawing room (page 34). The top swag was painted freehand in the same colour using a 5 cm (2 in) decorator's brush.

way of printing stencils is to cut the garment out first, then lay each piece of the pattern flat, with the sleeves in the armholes, and fiddle around with the stencil until I have got the design exactly where I want it. In the case of the tiger it took ages to position the design so that the whole body fitted on to the coat. If you are not sure whether you are going to like the effect, I suggest you try printing it out on to calico before you use expensive material.

AFTER CARE

For years I have been dealing with hand-painted cloth and how to clean it. Recently I ran some tests to find out what happened to the paint when put through different cleaning methods.

I found that dry cleaning does not suit gold powders, as most of the metallic paint is removed by the solvent, and machine-washing has a similar effect. Hand-washing seems to be the answer. Cloth painted or stencilled with emulsion survives the hot programme in a washing machine but comes out antiqued. I think this is because the strong spin creases the cloth and forces it against the drum at high speed so cracking the paint. It is easy to avoid this by selecting the wool programme. Calico will shrink in the washing machine. If you are in any doubt, I suggest you follow my usual procedure, which is to fill the bath with hand-hot water, add a pure soap liquid, then put in the curtain or whatever and swish it around before leaving it to soak for a few hours. Move the cloth to the back of the bath, pull out the plug and leave the material to drain. If you are not satisfied that the cloth is clean enough give it another wash, otherwise refill the bath with hand-hot water, push the cloth around, empty the water out of the bath and repeat this until the water runs clear. Any soap left in the material will eventually rot it, so try to remove as much as you can. Leave the cloth to drain, then hang it out to dry. Hanging the material while it is wet precludes the need for ironing, unless you are manic about a perfect finish.

From Calico to Curtains

Transforming a Room from Start to Finish

The challenge was set when the owner of one of the larger Parisian firms informed me categorically that I was not a textile designer and should stick to walls. Needless to say he did not buy the collection of designs which I thought included some of my best ideas to date,

Fighting Tigers

At first I intended to use the fighting tiger design in my drawing room. Once I had water-marbled the paper and hung it and then finished the malachite, I printed up a sample tiger and stapled it to the wall. Replacing all the furniture, I left the sample hanging in the room for a couple of weeks. After walking in and out to view the effect, I soon found that it was really too much to live with, so the stencils were hung up and left until I could think of another way to use them.

wishing only to purchase wallpaper designs that he was not being offered. From the age of six I used every year to send my 'collection', on minuscule pieces of paper, to a textile manufacturer, who was kind enough to write back saying that the work was interesting and that they looked forward to the next set. As the idea never died I should be grateful to him for the encouragement he gave me.

Having just finished the kitchen wallpaper and gone to bed to regain strength for the next process, which was to be stencilled tigers parading round the lower half of the room (they never materialized), I awoke the next morning with the idea of proving to myself and my Frenchman that I could make cloth designs work. If I experimented on calico I could find out if I was a textile designer or not. The most important thing when starting a new venture is to eliminate any form of worry, especially that of ruining something expensive. Also I like to indulge my sense of extravagance by using as much cloth as I feel like at the time.

The fighting tiger stencils were already cut for the wallpaper idea (page 84) so I could go straight on to the next stage, which was to measure up the cloth. The calico I use is usually 150cm (60in) wide. I thought one and a half

Viewing the Effect

I used to use my hallway to store my stencils – many of them hung up on the wall – and to display rolls of decorated cloth. It was only when I started to print up the new curtains for this room that I stopped working in the kitchen and finally set up a proper work table which could cope with the 3.75 m (12 ft) lengths of cloth that I planned to stencil for the curtains.

widths would be enough and the ceiling drop was about 2.75m (9ft), so I cut the calico a metre (3ft) longer to allow for extra draping. You can always cut curtains shorter, but lengthening them is a different story (which I experienced once, years ago, and never want to repeat if I can help it).

Before printing I thought it would be best to make the curtains up, hems and all, so that if the pattern-matching was not quite exact it would not show on the seams. I gave the made-up curtains a quick iron to flatten any wrinkles or puckered hems.

I printed up the borders first in black emulsion, using the tiger stripe along the leading edge and the bottom. This gave me a guide line for stencilling the tigers – positioned in their fighting stance – which had to be repeated all the way down the 3.7m (12ft) length on each of the four pairs of curtains.

Pushing the Paint Through

Once the stencil is secured in position, the pattern is printed with undiluted black emulsion paint on a long-handled stencil brush using a swift stabbing motion.

Removing the Stencil

When the whole design has been stencilled, detach the masking tape and smoothly lift off the sheet of paper.

Printing the Repeat

Because I am too impatient to wait for the paint to dry properly, I often take a risk and very gingerly move the printed cloth to make room for the repeat.

Once I had finished the first curtain, I was so impatient to see the effect, as usual, that I could not resist hanging it up almost before the paint was dry. It worked, so I carried on with the rest of the job. The curtains were to be dress ones only, so I saw no need to attach heading tape. Pleating the top of each curtain in thirteen 5-7.5cm (2-3in) pleats, I quickly pushed the headings through the sewing machine to hold everything in place. Then, with a staple gun, I fixed the curtains to the wall above the window. Holding the outside edge of the curtain two-thirds of the way down, I stapled that edge of the cloth in line with the heading to create a huge swag. This gave a dramatic and unusual style to the room. The fighting tigers took on an almost abstract quality, although on closer inspection you could still make out the animal shape. To

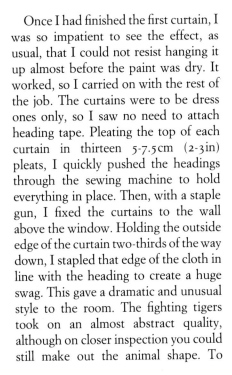

Flying Fur

The original idea for this design came from hours watching my cats engaging in mock battles. On the left is the submissive tiger with the fighting tiger facing him.

neaten off the curtain headings, I sewed lengths of calico into tubes, which I then ruched up and stapled to the wall. Each end of this extra heading was finished with a printed rosette (page 126). I added one in the middle, embellished with two silk dressing gown cords.

Thinking I had finished the job I picked up the telephone to invite my brother's criticism. I should have known better: 'Wonderful, it really works, why don't you print up a tablecloth to complement the whole effect, then you can invite us all for supper?' Great idea. Out came the sewing machine and the whole procedure started again. From there the idea seemed to grow: next, cushion covers, then a commission to design table mats, culminating in a trip to New Covent Garden to buy the finishing touch – cacti and pots – at five in the morning.

Moment of Truth

Once I had finished all the printing I could not resist hanging up the new look while waiting for the last curtain to dry (left). At least the room would be back to normal for a little while. The work table was turned into a dining table and laid for a celebration meal (above). On the director's chairs are cushions stencilled with the head of the same tiger.

Tigers on the Table

Once the curtains and swags were finished, I was persuaded to make a cloth to cover the work table (overleaf). First I sewed the calico together and turned up the hem. Then I placed it on the table and marked exactly where the border should go along the top edge with a soft pencil. I stencilled a tiger-rug tiger (used on a chair in the kitchen, page 85) while the cloth was in position, leaving the rest of the surface unprinted so that the tiger-stripe table mats would be clearly seen. Then I printed the border and sides. Lastly I stencilled a couple of cushions before the stencil finally fell apart.

DESIGNS
and stencils

Striped Tiger

This is another variation of the tiger design. This time I have cut out a stencil so that the tiger has a contrasting colour for the body, to make the stripes more clearly defined, and clouds have been interspersed between the main design. Marbled paper can be over-printed with any stencils – even small designs such as shells. African pots and plants figure largely here and they have always been a significant influence in my textile designs.

Portuguese Blue-and-White

I received for my birthday a wonderful book on Portuguese interiors. This, along with a strong Chinese influence, was to set the scene for the redecoration of the house once the builders had eventually moved out. The whole house seemed to have suffered, looking rather like a worn-out stage set. There is a difference between planned antiquing and the real bashed-up look. All the carpets had to be thrown out for a start, because they were full of cement and lime mortar dust, which seemed to have percolated everywhere despite having dust sheets over all the doors.

The first step in redecorating was to blank out all the old decorations with white. Having stated once that I never used white paint, especially in English houses, I was so overcome by the light, clean effect of the white walls that at first I could hardly even think of covering them up. But my obsession with stencilling was just beginning.

As I pored over my new book, reflecting that I could be living in Portugal instead of this windy cold climate, it occurred to me that I already had some furniture – an Indo-Portuguese sofa, a gilded mirror and table, and a Charles II Chinese cabinet on stand – which was so similar in style to the furniture shown in the Portuguese interiors that perhaps I could create my own private Portugal right here in London.

The newly laid black-and-white tiled floor started to give that colonial feeling, while I toyed with the idea of hand-painting tiles to clad the walls. On having a closer look at the room's defects, I decided that the walls were so uneven and had sagged to such an

Blind to Imperfections

I stencilled the Roman blinds with the top portion of the dado design. As I had not planned to carry the design on to the cloth when stencilling the room, the pattern did not match at the edges with that on the wall, but nobody has ever remarked on this discrepancy.

Improvising the Door Surround

When I had finished painting the room I felt that the door (opposite) needed to be made to look grander. I remembered that I had cut a stencil some years before to decorate the study door, which could perhaps be re-used with some slight modifications. Having spent hours trying to find my safe hiding place, I was delighted when I found the stencil and that my memory had served me correctly. Using large quantities of masking tape to block out parts of the design I could not fit over the door, I managed to eke out the nearly finished paint mix.

extent that the tiles could end up looking like a hotch-potch, because in order to fit round the room they would have had to be cut all over the place. Also I did have to think of the expense, and tiles are not exactly the cheapest method of redecorating a room. I made up my mind that I could not possibly paint out the clouded ceiling which seemed to work so well in the room, quite apart from having been achieved with suffering. I was not quite ready to let it go, so I had to choose a colour that would complement the ceiling. Since blue is one of my favourite colours, and evoked thoughts of blue-and-white Chinese ceramics imported by the Portuguese during the seventeenth century, I thought that a sort of slate blue, stencilled on to white, would be the perfect colour combination.

The first stage in the design was to draw the portion above the dado, which has a repeat every 1.2m (4ft). Because the room seems to have several focal points I thought that the best way to arrange the design was to centre it on the three main walls, making sure that the fireplace was treated symmetrically. Fortunately the corners seemed to solve their own problems. I carried the design over the two Roman blinds, and although the design did not match perfectly on the edges somehow nobody seemed to notice. The next part of the design to be cut and stencilled was the skirting board (base board), which echoed the squirls and acanthus leaf pattern of the top section.

The middle section gave the most problems, for some reason. I felt that if I covered the whole room with acanthus leaves the effect would be too heavy,

Chinese Symbols

Having had to sell all my Elizabethan oak collection in order to pay for my architect's extravagances, I was left with no bedroom furniture except a mattress on the floor. This was not uncomfortable, but felt rather bleak after all my fantasies of grandeur. One morning my mother phoned to say that the most

The Divine Chinese Monster

My bed was installed before I had decided what decoration to use on the walls. Eventually I was inspired by two Chinese vases painted with symbols and flowers. The blind was made with slats attached to the front of it, so producing a more authentic Chinese flavour, and designs were stencilled across it to match the walls.

exotic bed was to be auctioned that afternoon: did I want to rush over to the sale room and view it? There was one slight problem – its size. It was almost as large as the room. On viewing, I decided instantly that come what may it was for me. About an hour later I became the proud owner of this divine monster.

I must admit that when it was delivered I thought I had really bitten off more than I could chew this time. It took up the whole floor area of my entrance hall. The removal men had only just managed to get the base through the front door, so how was I to negotiate the staircase, which had presented so many problems in the past? Right up until the day when the cabinet-maker arrived to put it back together I tried unsuccessfully to palm the bed off on to anybody who showed the slightest interest. One look at this huge quantity of lacquered and gilded wood, and the answer was always the same: no.

The big day arrived, and fortunately for me a dealer friend dropped in unexpectedly and was able to take over the operation, showing the cabinet-maker how to get the bed apart and then helping him to carry it upstairs and put the whole enormous structure back together again. I was left to organize copious cups of coffee and tea.

As I lounged back in this magnificent bed, hoping that all who had turned it down would now regret their lost opportunity, I still felt totally defeated when it came to deciding what decoration would be suitable for the room. I had immediately discovered that any other piece of furniture, save my brass-bound chest, looked dwarfed when near the bed. Whatever the design was to be, it would have to stand up in its own right. A week passed and I was no nearer the answer. Then suddenly one night, just before turning out the light, I remembered two early nineteenth-century Chinese vases I had seen among my friend's imported stock. The next morning I phoned her and the vases were delivered the following day. I started drawing up my designs straightaway, and within hours of the vases arriving was cutting the stencils. I needed more symbols than were portrayed on the vases, so all available books were spread over the floor. The

A Galaxy of Symbols

Although I repeated symbols, I made a rule that each design could only be printed out twice on any one wall. The colour of paint which I mixed is a very dark brown/red, or sang de boeuf, which matches the lacquer of the bed almost perfectly. In order to achieve vases that were perfectly symmetrical I only drew one half, then, during stencilling, once the paper was dry, I turned it over and carefully matched it up with the other side.

whole pattern was made up of 35 or 40 different symbols, so that each did not have to be repeated more than twice.

I mixed a paint colour to complement the lacquer of the bed – a very dark, almost black, ox-blood red – and then turned my attention to the window blind. Because the bed stood in front of the window the blind was thrown into prominence as a backdrop. Instead of fitting the wooden slats at the back, as is usual with Roman blinds, I felt it would look more in keeping to put them on the front and colour them dark red. To deceive the eye further, I stencilled the blind with the same paint as was used on the walls. I printed up the bed linen using only the fan motif, and this time used proper fabric dye. This worked well on the pure cotton duvet cover, but gave considerable difficulty by bleeding on the polyester-cotton mix of the pillow slips. Also, after a few washes it began to fade, although every precaution was taken to fix the dye permanently.

I reaped considerable pleasure from the decorative effects in this room where, for all the size of the bed, the atmosphere was light and airy.

The Dragon Room

I wanted to keep to a mainly white theme in this phase of redecoration, because I had discovered that the light played quite different games on a white background, and the house seemed to remind me more and more of my childhood home in Nigeria. I had just bought another Chinese mandarin's bed: a single one which I liked rather more than the huge marriage bed I had acquired some three weeks earlier and placed in the larger bedroom. This room was planned not to have much furniture: the bed, an antique Thai elephant chair and a blue-and-white Chinese stool. The decoration could therefore be as outrageous as I wanted to make it. It occurred to me that one of my blue-and-white vases would look wonderful enlarged on the walls, and I decided to draw up a design of dragons chasing the pearl of wisdom running round the room, frolicking among foaming waves, with stylized Chinese clouds scattered at random.

So started a week of torture to my poor hands. Having drawn up the dragon's head I discovered that, as often seems to happen in my case, I had scaled it up to huge proportions, forgetting that the body would have to follow suit. Ten sheets later I eventually saw the tip of his tail. Because there seemed to be furniture strewn all over the house, with all the comings and goings of changing old pieces for different ones needing mending or recovering, there was not enough space to lay out the whole stencil, so I was not to see the dragon complete in one piece until it was on the wall. Clearly by then there was no going back. I'm not sure what I would have done if I hadn't liked it.

Blind, Curtain and Wall

To carry the dragon design round the room I had to print the stencil over both the blind and the curtains and then on to the wall. I printed the dragon's head on to the blind first, then I laid the curtain flat and lined up the stencil to join the body and head. Once the blind and curtains were hung, I printed out the tail on the wall.

The Dragon That Did Not Fit

I designed a different head for the body of the dragon opposite, but after hours of painstaking cutting, they did not fit together. I overcame this problem by carefully drawing up the missing shapes and using an artist's fitch to stipple the paint into place. The stylized Chinese clouds were cut on individual pieces of stencil paper and scattered above the dragons and all over the ceiling, while the foaming waves served as a dado. The design originated from one of my blue-and-white Chinese vases and proved to be one of the largest stencils I have ever cut, measuring 4.46m (14ft 6in) in length.

While I was bent over the cutting board the painter went round blanking out the previous designs on the walls. Eventually we were both finished, and I began the first print-out of the dragon. I had cut out the curling waves, with a repeat that ran to 1.2m (4ft), and positioned them along the top of the skirting board, stencilling them in a flat middle blue – I did not want the waves to detract from the main feature.

On finishing the first dragon, I decided that the next one should not only change colour slightly, but should also have a different head, facing his opponent as though they were playing a game of who could grab the pearl first. The new head was cut and I thought I had matched it to the body with care, but when it was stencilled on to the wall and I tried to match up the original body I found that somehow there seemed to be rather a large area which was mismatched. My decision was pretty instant: I was not going to spend hours recutting any part of that scaly beast, as my hands were already in a dreadful state. I lined up the next portion to fit as best I could and stencilled the darker blue paint on. The rest of the body followed swiftly, leaving me to fill in the 45cm (18in) gap between head and body. With a pencil I faintly drew in the missing scales, then, using a fitch with almost no paint and keeping the bristles as dry as I could, I stippled the colour in place. On standing back, I noted with satisfaction that you could hardly see the difference between the stencilled and hand-painted portions.

Encouraged by this, I decided that the third dragon could sport a new tail. Preparing the stencil paper to the size I

47

wanted, I printed out the old tail, which belonged to the second dragon, then interwove the new tail round it, curling and looping like the coils of a snake. I intended to put the head of this dragon on the blind and the body on the curtains and the walls. I thought it was more sensible to start off by printing the blind and curtains before printing the body on to the walls. The curtains were made and ready to hang, so having stencilled the head on the blind and left it to dry, I laid the right-hand curtain out flat and proceeded to line up the body section exactly. When this was dry I hung the curtain so that I could pattern-match the rest of the body and tail on the wall. The left-hand curtain was stencilled with the dragon's paw, with clouds added as on the other curtain. These were in a lighter colour than the waves, and were scattered above the dragons and over the ceiling to create a feeling of space.

Now the room was complete and the furniture was in place, with the lacquered bed positioned in front of the window (I had tried it against the long wall, but it ended up giving a railway carriage effect and hiding most of the dragon). On seeing that the dragon covered the entire wall, I began to wonder how long he really was: I could hardly believe it when I found he was 4.46m (14ft 6in) long.

One day, when a friend asked where the pearl of wisdom was, it suddenly dawned on me that I had not printed out this all-important feature. The stencil had been designed and cut but where was it? I confess that events overtook me; the pearl was never found and another never cut.

Scaling Up

Here we have a picture of as much of the dragon as could be fitted in. When I started I did not imagine that the beast would grow to such immense proportions, but the body grew and grew to balance the head.

Turkish Broken Tulip

It was around the time of the buying of the Chinese beds that I happened to pop my nose into the Oriental Ceramics Sale, and saw a plate which I would dearly have loved to buy – but for once I reminded myself that there were other more important things needed and managed to abstain. On browsing through a catalogue some time later I

The Virtues of Compromise

This bathroom (below) is a good illustration of how you sometimes have to compromise. The central medallion in the dado has no outer border. It was fortunate that such a small sacrifice solved the problem of making it all fit. I stencilled the door (opposite) with an old border never used before. Luckily there was a suitable break in the design so it exactly fitted the lower panels.

came across a similar plate, described as mid-sixteenth century and decorated with a design based on tulips. As I have a passion for tulips my imagination sprang into action. There must be a room that this design would enhance.

My main bathroom has no windows, so I have tried to disguise this by creating the illusion of sitting on a

balcony. The idea was inspired by our bathroom in Nigeria, where the windows opened flat against the outside walls, allowing the branches of the flame tree to reach right into the room. From the bath you had a view over the garden to the lagoon beyond. Having just finished reading a book about India, where filigree and pierced stonework play such an important part in the architecture, I wondered whether I could also simulate this idea. In preparation I drew and cut tulip-pattern stencils for the dado to be repeated on the capstone of each column.

My first step was to paint the mural. Against a wash of blues, to suggest a windswept sky, I added my favourite tree, a magnolia, brought to Britain from China in the early nineteenth century. The branches were hand-painted in shades of dark brown, and the paint was sponged off in places to give the impression of light striking the wood here and there. With a fine pencil brush I outlined the entire trunk and all the branches in black, adding lumps and creases to the trunk and larger branches to simulate bark. The flowers were stencilled using white and yellow ochre picked up on the sponge at random. Next I added the birds, painting in the feathers with the same brush; and last came the bamboo, stencilled in dead-green paint, its fronds just poking over the top of the dado.

The height of the dado was marked out with charcoal, and the space below painted flat blue, leaving gaps for the columns which were added in white. Then the broken tulip design was stencilled on, using white straight out of the tin and making sure it faded in places. The tops of the columns were then printed in the same blue as the dado background, and the blue design of the columns was hand-painted with a fitch. A further stencil was cut to run round the ceiling, binding the columns together. Then the whole pattern was outlined in black, using the pencil brush

The Asymmetrical Ceiling

Although I measured from the centre point of the ceiling to an outer edge I forgot that it was not square, but having spent hours cutting this stencil out of acetate, I had no intention of starting again. I made a central rose to cover up the mistake, but the asymmetrical effect grew on me so it was never glued up.

The Technique in Detail

This bird detail shows in close-up how the effect was achieved. First I stencilled the different colours by masking off portions of the design, and then I hand-painted in the details using a pencil brush. The bamboo spikes were added as an afterthought when I came across them in the store room.

as before. I still felt the dado needed pulling together more, so I added a black line to echo the stencilled design.

Having got this far I decided that the ceiling should also have a stencilled pattern. As it was, the walls of the room looked rather like the filling in a sandwich. It was Christmas time, and as I went round the art shops I was to discover that they had run out of stencil paper in all sizes. They suggested that I try using acetate, which comes in much larger sheets than stencil paper. I did not like the look of it very much, but had no choice.

On arriving home I settled down to draw up the ceiling design, which was triangular in shape. I quickly discovered one plus; if you made a mistake with the felt pen a damp rag washed off the ink very easily. When it came to cutting I was less convinced. It was much harder to cut than paper, and when the knife slipped, which with me was every few minutes, I nearly cut half my hand off. I had a choice between waiting until after the public holidays, when I would be able to buy my usual materials, or finishing the stencil there and then. I chose the latter. On holding the finished stencil up, I realized that there was no possibility of getting a good registration on the ceiling. The way I had cut the design, half the middle fell out when it was still on the vertical, let alone upside down. Out came the lining paper. I gave it two coats of white emulsion and left it to dry, then stencilled the tulips on to it in the same blue as I had used in the rest of the room. Three more sections followed, then I painted a 2.5cm (1in) blue border round each section, edging them in black with the pencil brush.

Even though I had measured them carefully, when the printed triangles were hung up the effect was different from my original idea. The panels were to have met symmetrically in the centre, but somehow this did not happen. But I decided to leave them as they were, as it all looked rather stylish.

Chinese Cherry Blossom

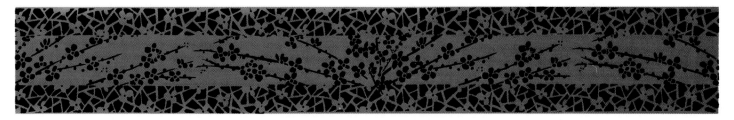

The use of cherry blossom is usually associated with the Japanese Edo period, from 1615-1868, but in fact it was a reproduction of a far earlier Chinese idea. The blue and white of much Chinese art has the uncanny quality of never tiring the eye, and always

Theme and Variations

When I had stencilled the dados and border I decided to treat the door (left) slightly differently, using a variation on the main theme. I edged the blinds (below) with printed calico, matching the top with the border on the wall so that it ran on uninterrupted.

appearing fresh. I also have a large collection of Adirẹ cloth brought back from Nigeria, which I trot out for use every so often, then wash and pack away for the next theme. Now I decided it was time to use it in the kitchen, with a blue-and-white stencilled design.

Simulated Tiles

As I do not like tiles on worktops and I thought the best idea was to print the cherry blossom pattern in squares to simulate tiles, I did not change the wall tiles (right), which I had painted some years before because I was still fond of the design.

After the Party

The kitchen table is drawn into the centre of the room when I give supper parties. After everyone had gone home on this occasion (below), my brother suggested I should leave the setting exactly as it was until a photograph could be taken.

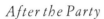

The first part of the room to evolve was the top border. This has two designs – symmetrically arranged cherry blossoms in the middle flanked by more blossom and twigs – I refer to it as 'broken plate'. The dado was influenced by the wooden slatted fencing used in China, which Chippendale later adapted to decorate his furniture during his Chinese Chippendale period.

In order to keep the design as light as possible, I broke up the solid slats with more cherry blossom and twigs, with birds feeding among the boughs. The upright supports carried on the same theme, while at the same time lending solidity to the dado. The door repeated the main border pattern, and the panels had cherry blossoms strung along elongated branches. Over the lintel I added a panel of blossom sprays to increase the perceived height of the door, thus making it more imposing. The last stencil, 15 cm (6 in) square, was to be used in a repeat pattern on the worktop to simulate tiles. I have never used real tiles on kitchen surfaces since an occasion in Mexico when I broke nearly all the household china (which had one advantage, as I was swiftly steered away from the kitchen and sent off to do something else).

The split cane blinds were off the peg, slightly personalized by me. Finding a piece of hardboard of the right size, I laid each blind flat on it in turn, then painted both sides with runny brown paint on a large 18 cm (7 in) brush, making sure that the paint went into all the cracks. Once they were dry I edged the blinds with calico, hand-printed to match the border above the picture rail. This was a long and arduous job. Finally I made two printed ties to which to attach the tassels.

Several variations on the basic Chinese fence theme have been cut but never used. Nevertheless, they show how one design can be used in different ways to give a room a completely new lease of life.

African Animals

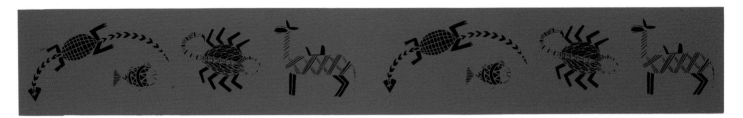

The majority of African designs are usually geometrical. When used with a wide range of colours the patterns take on quite a different appearance. Although the basic construction of these stylized animals makes up a pattern which is essentially geometrical,

The Garden Door

The carving over the garden door, although baroque in style, blended with the dark purple glazed cotton – a fortunate find, even if at first I could not imagine where to use it. The African animals were stencilled on to the made-up curtains in scarlet emulsion.

the nature of the overall design suggested to me that they would look more sophisticated stencilled in a single colour. Each animal or symbol represents the wildlife and tools in and around African villages. These designs are traditionally carved on chieftain's doors, or on furniture and pottery.

I cut over 30 symbols, together with a border. The curtains for which the design was intended were of dark aubergine glazed chintz. I always make up curtains and blinds before printing them (page 125) because I like to be able to stencil over the seams, and to the very edges of the hem and sides. There were six curtains to be covered with animals. Although it is more usual to make sets of curtains so that they are identical with each other, for this particular design it seemed to me better to spread the animals and symbols round, so that each one had a chance not to be lost in the folds when the cloth was drawn back. The border was printed along the bottom of each curtain length only.

The pair of curtains which hang on the garden door needed extra decoration below the carving. I was really lucky to find a bolt of striped silk of the sort used for ties: although rather rotten it was a wonderful colour match, with a line of scarlet on the selvedge which picked up the red of the animals. I pushed it into place, the stripes forming twists and turns as the cloth wriggled behind the carving. Rosettes (page 126) added the final touch.

Inspiration for the Designs

One of my sources of ideas for the animals was this African Abuja pot (right).

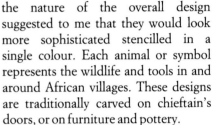

African Plants and Pots

Having spent many years in Africa, my designs have often been influenced by the plants and designs that are characteristic of West Africa.

I was asked by one of my brothers to help refurbish his upstairs landing. Because the area has large windows on two sides, facing east and north, I chose to use undyed calico for the curtains which would keep the landing light. To give a feeling of an exotic garden room I

African Landing

I stencilled several variations of terracotta pots combined with plants, flowers and cacti (right) which my brother liked and wanted incorporated in his redecoration (below). To suggest more of the African style planned for the new curtains I replaced the carpet with rush matting and then put a camel-hair blanket – brought back from the Cameroons – on the sofa with new cushion covers edged in cowrie shells. The green of the cacti picked up one of the stripes in the blanket.

decided to decorate them with cacti planted in earthenware pots. I cut out several types of cacti stencils, mixed a terracotta-coloured paint for the pots and chose a dead green for the plants, a colour which picked up one of the stripes in the African blanket.

The curtains were hung giving the exotic effect I had hoped for. All that was needed to complete the African illusion were masses of lush green plants

which we gathered together from other parts of the house.

Because the upstairs landing was so successful, my brother then asked me to decorate his dining room. The design was heavily influenced by Shoowa textiles from the kingdom of Kuba now part of Zaire. I incorporated several designs to make up the dado and, by turning the stencil upside down on alternate printouts, the repeat was lengthened from 61cm to 122cm (2ft to 4ft). For the walls, I chose to use natural calico once again. I sewed this up and printed over the seams just as in the bathroom, then stapled it to the walls in the usual way (page 122).

While the stencil brushes were still wet with terracotta paint, I first used a natural sponge dipped in the terracotta to give a soft background to the cushion covers, then printed a pot on to the centre of each cover. These were edged with a simple geometric border. The table napkins were treated in the same way. This continuation of the design linked this room with the others.

My brother was fortunate to find a modern glass table in a sale room. This keeps the room simple, allowing you to see the design through the base, and sets off a collection of Abuja pottery to perfection. The flooring was chosen to match the landing area upstairs.

African Dining

One of the advantages of the glass table in my brother's dining room is that the pattern on the dado is not obscured. I replaced the chairs with Nigerian stools. They were made more comfortable by adding stencilled cushions; the pot design tied in with the other rooms. Abuja pottery, a statue from northern Nigeria and some of my paintings – one of which incorporates the African animal stencils – helped to complete the decoration.

The third room I decorated was my brother's bathroom – covering up the exotic marbling I had previously painted. I knew it would take several coats of white paint to obliterate the intense blue, so I suggested that it would be quicker and cheaper to stretch printed calico over the walls.

First I sewed the lengths of natural-coloured cloth together so that I could print over the seams. Then, using a different selection of pot stencils, I printed each one in terracotta, immediately adding philodendron leaves before printing the next pot. By printing the loosely constructed pattern

Philodendron Bathroom

I printed the same philodendron leaf stencil throughout the design for the bathroom wall-covering and the curtains, but the accompanying pot stencils were changed to alter the height and positioned so that the leaves would cover the largest possible area of the walls.

in this way I achieved maximum coverage, so that the exotic leaves remained the centre of attention.

Once the cloth was stapled to the walls (page 122) I was able to decide how I would treat the window. Because it already had a red roller blind which I was not allowed to change, the only solution was to make up a pair of dress curtains in calico. I printed these using a variety of pots, then added the philodendron leaves and some amaryllis lilies which introduced a touch of red to complement the blind and gave a dash of colour to the otherwise green and terracotta decoration.

Tiled Gallery

At last my gallery had been built. Now I could fulfil a dream that had lasted for nearly a year and a half. When I had first thought of incorporating the cellars into the main part of the house, I had already planned to use a tiled dado. I had measured out the wall areas as I thought

An Exotic Paradise

Once the builders had left, it was up to me to decorate the gallery. The hand-painted cut-out was nailed in place over the alcove and the wooden mouldings were fixed to the top of the pond after it had been lined with tiles stencilled with a carnation motif.

they would be, then started to paint hundreds of tiles. I wanted to create the effect of looking over a stone balustrade to a garden below. Between the stone pillars you would glimpse exotic fruits, flowers in vases, peacocks and other birds of all sorts.

Once I had actually embarked on this escapade I soon decided to make the whole scheme more of a challenge. Each vase of flowers and bowl of fruit would be of a different species and as botanically correct as I could paint them. Some of the birds were also anatomically accurate but others were pure fantasy. The peacocks would be stylized, based on my childhood memories of our peacocks in Lagos. To unify the whole design I chose shades of blue-grey against the white background of the tiles. This scene took up four rows of tiles, and a further two were decorated with a stencilled motif of acanthus leaves, which served as the ledge and the capstones to the pillars.

I cut a stencil for the columns to ensure that each one was the same shape and size, but only used it to trace the outline. Then I filled the centre in by hand and sponged off the onglaze to give a freckled finish and eliminate any brush marks. The black line round the edge of the column was softened by pushing the wet brush up to the inner edge, making sure that the line remained sharp on the outside. The blue line which joins the columns at the top and bottom was measured and marked out then painted and sponged. After it was dry I cleaned off any mistakes with cotton buds.

To stave off the boredom of producing hundreds of stencilled tiles I would view the middle portion as my treat: once I had painted a certain number of acanthus leaves I was allowed to have fun with the flowers and birds.

I think the whole dado took nearly six weeks to paint and fire. I found that the antiquing, for which I used both methods (page 21) almost took longer than the original painting. The tiler made a magnificent job of matching up all the designs. Thank goodness I had kept a record of the order I had painted the scenes in, as the final space had changed quite a bit from my first plans:

The Instant Cupola

My builder only allowed me three days to design and paint the gallery ceiling before the floor was pulled out. The plaster was still damp but there was nothing else I could do if (as I did) I wanted to simulate a cupola. The sky was painted in emulsion and rubbed down with fine sandpaper when dry. The ellipse was painted in pale grey, then stencilled with gold powders to suggest fancy gilded plasterwork. The border of leaves and berries was added to the perimeter of the circle as an afterthought and so had to slip down the side of the ceiling on two sides.

luckily there were hardly any alterations to be made.

In order to make the antiqued tiles resemble old ones I asked the tiler to grout them in grey because the old-fashioned way of hanging them was with cement. Another advantage of not grouting in white is that you do not have to keep bleaching the joints which usually become yellowed with age.

Once the pond had been tiled on the outside and the cut-out pinned to the wall, I thought that the back part of the pond, aptly named by some the 'black hole of Calcutta', would benefit from being tiled. I had noticed that the sun reached quite far back into it, and so imagined that perhaps the tiles would reflect more light, bringing the back wall forward visually. To make the most of the tiles' reflective white background I chose a delicate Persian carnation design I had seen on a piece of cloth. Every alternate tile had a flower in the middle, a quarter of a star in each corner and a thin line round the edge. The tiles without flowers had the star sections to match up with the others and the edging line. My idea worked beautifully: the sun reflected from the water, which is always moving, and plays a dappled light on the walls. An antique Indian rice bowl holds tiny Chinese goldfish and overflows with water which splashes into the main pond, where larger fish weave slowly in and out, coming to the surface at feeding time.

Peacocks and Pomegranates

The dado runs round the whole gallery, even into the tiny courtyard at the back of the building, and the design is made up of a collection of hand-painted exotic fruits, flowers and birds with borders of stencilled acanthus leaves. There are nearly 2,000 tiles altogether, which is why I chose to stencil the borders above and below the main design. The idea was to create the feeling that you were looking through a stone balustrade.

Fighting Tigers

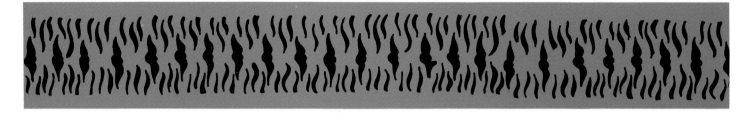

The first time I saw the Tibetan tiger rugs I immediately had an insatiable desire to have these ferocious beasts all over the house. I quickly discovered that they lent themselves amazingly well to be used in stencil form. There were no

The Tiger Rug

Instead of printing the fighting tigers on the walls, as planned, I stencilled them on to a rush mat, which they instantly transformed. Cushion covers in black and gold also show portions of the tiger's body.

worries about bridges or 'legs', and not only did the whole design hang together, but it also looked really dramatic, seeming to enhance anything it was printed on.

The idea at first was to use the more

stylized tiger on a dado, accompanied by either Tibetan flowers or clouds. The first thing to do was to marble the paper (page 20) which I had decided to use as a backdrop to the design. It also meant that I did not have to blank out the previous decoration, which I knew would take me or someone else hours; papering was instant. A friend was persuaded to come over to the house and teach me how to hang paper, something I knew how to do but have never actually done. I felt now was the time to learn. Then my friend suggested that I sit down and carry on with my designs while she put the wallpaper up, as it would be quicker, and did I really feel it was necessary to learn to hang paper when others could do the job for me? I did not take much persuading.

Everything happened so quickly that I did not even have time to say goodbye to the Chinese fence which had given me so much pleasure. There wasn't time to be sad, as I was overtaken by excitement at the new look which was spreading rapidly over my walls. Instead of hanging the paper in the normal manner, I had it hung horizontally. This is usually done when the walls are in such a bad condition that two layers of paper are hung to make sure that the surface is as smooth as possible. This treatment gave the marbled paper a totally different look. It reminded me of Rome, with huge blocks of pale amber marble or sandstone, and made the room look grand and enormously tall.

While the paper was being hung I practised printing the tigers and flowers on to some of the marbled paper, so that I could pin it up before actually putting brush to paper on the kitchen walls. By the evening most of the kitchen had been redecorated and the furniture was back in position. I had an early night in order to be fresh for a good day's stencilling. Suddenly, at three in the morning, I woke with a start. I wandered down to the kitchen for a glass of water, then I just sat gaping into

The Made-to-Measure Tiger

This particular tiger (above) was specially designed and cut to fit the planter's chair, although later on I could not resist using it elsewhere. I specifically printed the yellow cloth in black only because the cushions had been stencilled in black and over-printed with gold to make more of a contrast. On the back of the chair (top) – which faces the door – I used the flower design to provide an element of surprise for visitors when they came into the room.

space and admiring this new decorative effect. What a shame I was going to spoil it with stencils.

It suddenly occurred to me that I was about to launch into a repeat version of the last decoration. Why not leave the walls plain and put all the stencilled patterns on to cloth? Down came the dado, never to be used. The next morning saw the start of a new obsession which was to possess me for the next few months. Out came the cloth and packets of yellow dye, and while waiting for the cloth to dry I practised stencilling the black emulsion on to lengths of undyed material. The effect was pleasing, smart, but somehow *déjà vu.* What would happen if gold powders were stencilled over the black? The mixture of several shades of gold was fantastic.

By that evening every piece of dyed cloth had been covered with golden flowers, tigers and clouds. This was the answer. Out came the sewing machine to run up cushion covers. I was almost frantic to see this new look finished and worked halfway through the night, until samples and cushions adorned every corner of the room.

The cushions were printed out with portions of the newest stencil of the fighting tigers which I had only just cut. Seeing that they looked good, I thought that the planter's chair deserved a specially made-to-measure tiger. This was cut and stencilled in black only, leaving the gold-flowered covers to catch the sunlight. The back of the chair, which faces you as you enter, was upholstered with ungilded flowers, giving no clue of what was to follow.

So as not to abandon the first tiger stencils I transferred the dado design on to the table-cloth, which is left in place all the time, more for decorative than for practical purposes. I also used the fighting tigers on the rush matting, which I found to be a good way of making an ordinary cheap mat look stylish and expensive.

Tigers on Cushions ...

This chair (above) was put back into working order by replacing the once-upholstered seat with plywood. I had intended to mend it properly but ran out of time, so instead I simply covered the plywood with cloth printed with black and gold carnations. A tiger-printed pillow makes it more comfortable.

... And on Table-Cloths

Once I had made up my mind not to print any stencils on to the walls I dyed metres of calico in yellow. I started off by making cushions printed with tigers and flowers, and then moved on to the table-cloth (right), using the tigers that had been designed for the dado.

The cloth has proved very practical even though I had my fears about washing the red flowers as red is not very stable and often presents problems. I soon discovered that if the machine was set on a wool wash the paint did not run or fade.

Persian Ribbons and Carnations

The drawing room was hung with water-marbled paper between the picture rail and the dado. Above and below I had pasted up paper painted with fantasy malachite. Lastly some bright spark had suggested quartering the ceiling with marbled paper, which gave the paperhanger neck ache for several days afterwards. The furniture was replaced with an old red Persian carpet

Persian Jewels

The red chair (left) echoes the Persian carpet and gives colour to this predominantly grey and green room with black-and-gold cloth to give a jewel-like quality. The room (below) draws together nearly all the different stencils used throughout the house. The only pattern not repeated elsewhere is the Persian ribbon design used to swag the blinds. Several shades of gold were printed to make the cloth shimmer.

which I had found in the store, covered in moth. It had needed scrubbing and was shoved in the drawing room to make sure it dried out properly. There it was destined to stay.

Now that the bones of the room were complete I decided to go to town on the cloth. First of all I took the Roman blinds down and gave them two or three coats of emulsion. I thought it was a

waste to throw them out as there really was nothing wrong with them, and if the paint made the cloth too stiff then I could think again. Just before rehanging them I stencilled the tiger stripe border in gold powders along the bottom edge. Once back in place the blinds seemed to work, so I set about preparing the cloth for ruched pelmets (page 126).

My collection of antique Turkish cushions was to be kept on the sofa. Clearly the main cover had to be changed, so sorting through piles of cloth I found some left-over black cotton damask, of which there was only just enough. This I stencilled up with the Persian carnation design which had been used in the kitchen on my free

Georgian Restoration

This Georgian chair was quickly covered with the aid of pins though it could, of course, be sewn for a more permanent finish. The Tibetan flowers were stencilled in the same green used for the malachite background on to black damask, which looks very rich because you are stencilling over a woven flower design which can be seen when the light strikes the cloth.

chair and cushions. On visiting the East End of London I was lucky to find more black damask which seemed to have come off the same roll as that used on the sofa. Choosing the Tibetan flower design, I stencilled it in the background malachite green, printing up the amount of material needed to cover one of the Georgian chairs. The second chair was covered in a variation of the carnation design, this time in black on red with copper butterflies flitting in and out of the flower stems. Using some more of the damask, I then printed up a couple of cushions with the shell stencils I had used in the small bathroom (page 100), echoing the gold and black of the sofa and cushions.

94

Shells and Sand

I have a very small bathroom which measures just 1.8 × 1.2m (6ft × 4ft), into which I have managed to cram a 1.2m (4ft) sit-up-and-beg bath (which is quite comfortable as it is very deep, and I lie back with my feet carefully propped up on the splashback), a lavatory and a corner wash basin.

Overcome by the different effects that could be produced by water-marbling (page 20), I thought I would try it again. In order to give that feeling of real depth, I made sure that the paper was graduated in colour from dark to really light, as it can be on a clear day in Devon waters, when you can see the sand rippling and the sun penetrates the water and highlights the odd shell or

Sun and Sea

One evening, while I was looking at all the different effects that could be achieved with water-marbling, I was suddenly inspired to try stencilling a design over it. Reaching for the nearest stencils I printed a selection of shells in ox-blood red, then added a line down one side of the sheet of paper so that the unmatched marbling would not be so obvious when the paper was hung. Now, every time I walk into the small bathroom I have the feeling of being by the seaside on a sunny day, when you look through the water and see the rippled sand and shadows cast by the moving water over odd shells or a piece of seaweed lying on the bottom. The silver Venetian mirror on the back wall, with its fanned shell top and beaten design, glints as the light strikes it, adding to the watery effect.

strand of seaweed beneath the surface.

Once I had prepared my paper I could not wait to try out stencilling the shells. There would be no particular pattern repeat, but to avoid ending up with two of the same kind of shell next to each other I kept each finished piece next to the one I was printing, numbering each sheet so that the paper-hanger would know the order in which they should be hung. The 2.5cm (1in) wide line was added to camouflage the fact that the sand ripples did not match from one sheet to the next. This is optional. Even though I say it myself I was thrilled with this watery atmosphere, which was to set the scene for the bathroom upstairs.

Flying Fish and Octopus

On one of my little window-shopping expeditions to the East End of London, when I was showing some friends where to buy cheap cloth for Christmas decorations, I came across piles of coloured satins and taffetas. I am sure they had been there gathering dust since before the war, and some of the cloth had gone so stiff with age that it would have been almost unusable. My friends, politely muttering something to the effect that I was not supposed to be spending again and what could one possibly want that material for anyway, turned their backs on my find. As sometimes happens I actually paid attention, returning home without spending a penny, only to suffer the whole week, regretting my stupidity more and more. I had to have the cloth, come what may. I have never said my prayers so fervently or so often, willing God to leave my pile of cloth safely undiscovered.

The next Sunday, the earliest date I could return, saw me up and out early. The cloth was as I had left it, so I was able to sort through, buying hundreds of metres of wonderful material which I intended to use for something – I had not quite thought what, but the idea would come, I hoped.

During my frenzied week of waiting to return to the East End, I had visited the Victoria and Albert Museum to buy a book that I needed for research. Whenever I go there I can never resist looking at all the new publications and usually spending a fortune; this time I came across a book on Minoan pots – the only one I have seen of its kind – which illustrated the most wonderful octopus, flying fish and corals. I rushed

The Mysterious Depths of the Sea

This wonderful cloth inspired me to cut stencils of living sea creatures, which I printed in gold powders. The delicate shading from almost black to light turquoise gave the illusion of being under water. This was the first time I had ever put up cloth on walls, so I did not realize how much would be needed until I had measured the room. I had only just enough cloth to finish the job.

home with it and got out my strong magnifying glass to examine the details of the black-and-white photographs. A few hours later saw me drawing up and cutting out all the sea plants and creatures, octopus and flying fish. I thought it would complement the shell design of the small bathroom, but this time showing the creatures that actually inhabit the shells.

On my return from my shopping trip, I got out the cloth which shaded from black to pale turquoise, and without cutting it, started to print out all the sea creatures and shells. As I did not want to cut the material I thought I would drape it over the curtain pole on the landing, which had a lengthy drop from window to floor and would show off this exquisite cloth with its delicate gold stencils, rather like something out of King Solomon's temple.

Up went the curtain swags. They looked dreadful. I pushed and pulled, tugging the cloth here and there. Eventually I telephoned my brother who never worries about telling the truth. 'Put it up on the bathroom walls, it looks dreadful like that.' This piece of bald advice started me off upholstering walls (page 122) – which I may say is cleaner and quicker than wallpapering. Also, since I can do it myself, it is cheaper. Another nice thing about upholstering the walls is that you can just cover everything. This is what I did: straight over the radiator and the door panels and even the ogee mouldings. I probably got quite carried away.

It is now my pleasure, on having a bath, to lie back in luxury and daydream about the mysterious hidden depths of the sea.

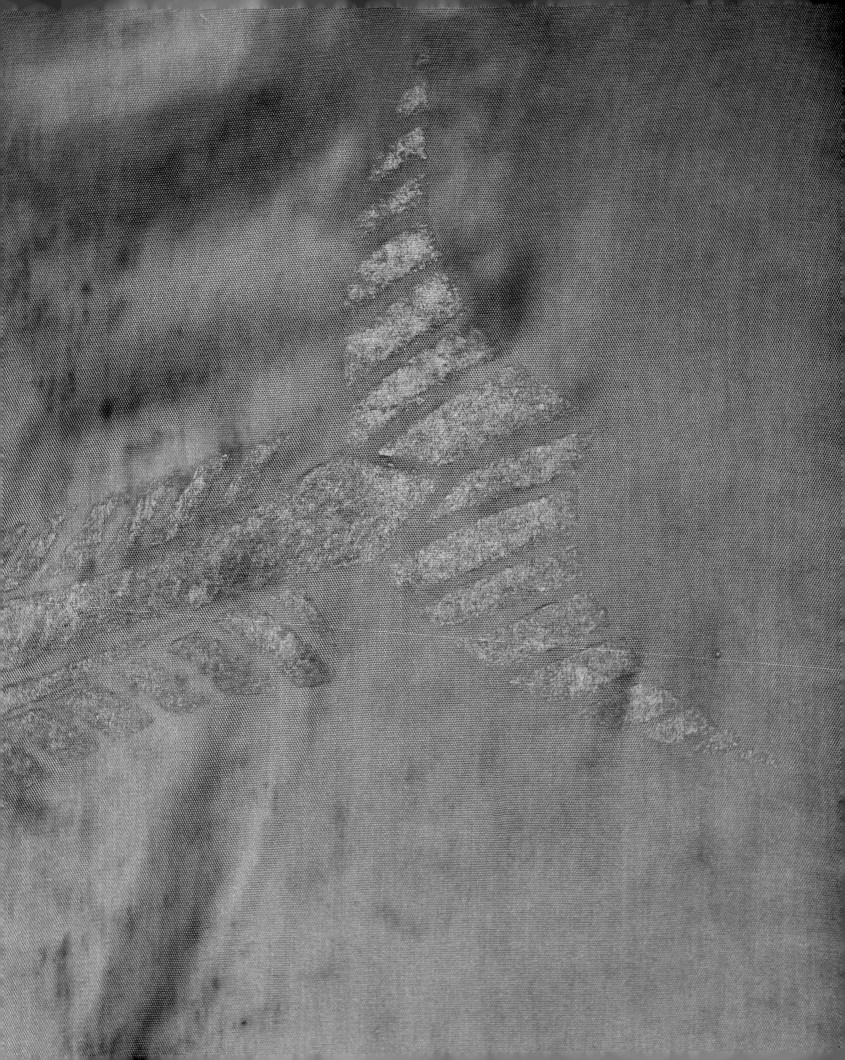

Waterlilies and Waves

Now that the water theme seemed to have crept up the stairs, I thought it should be used in all the other rooms on that floor, so that some sort of continuity prevailed. When I was buying the cloth that ended up in the large bathroom I had also acquired huge amounts of grey duchesse satin. Hours were spent measuring up the material to make sure that there was enough, as I had been

Swamped in Satin

Although this room is essentially Chinese in design it sometimes has a romantic atmosphere which reminds me of Bali. The candlestick is Indian, and the soft light makes the satin cloth glow. I found that with cloth on the walls and ceiling the room was warmer than usual during the winter, and I can only presume that material serves as an extra insulation against dark wet days. The ornate mandarin's bed is surprisingly comfortable.

surprised by the amount needed for the bathroom (page 104). When I worked out exactly how much cloth would be required I saw instantly that it was going to be a very tight squeeze, with no room for error. I could not go back to the shop for more cloth, as I had bought all that was available. Gritting my teeth, I decided to go ahead none the less, determined not to make any mistakes.

I have an early nineteenth-century Chinese goose dish on which I keep my soap. I am not sure why the dish is so-called, but I like both the name and the decoration, which uses waterlilies or lotus flowers in an unusual way. Waterlilies are rather hackneyed as a motif, particularly as a symbol of the Far East but, undaunted, I imagined that perhaps I could give them a new lease of life. Because it is easier to handle shorter lengths of cloth or paper I measured the drop required, adding a few inches for mistakes, then cut the cloth and stacked it in the same order. This was important because of the colour variation.

The leaves and stems of the plants and the waves were stencilled in a medium gold powder, while for the flowers I chose a copper gold. At first I was afraid this might look rather tasteless, but it was already too late; I could not throw the piece of cloth aside and start afresh, so I just had to keep going. When one wall was finished, I sewed it together and stapled it up.

Distributing the Designs

I used three separate stencils in turn on each length of cloth for the walls, rotating the stencils to ensure the design was evenly distributed. Empty areas were deliberately left from time to time to give breathing space and let the eye relax. Each stencil is different, illustrating seed pods, flowers in full bloom, leaves and a variety of frothing waves.

Luck can often work on your side. What I had feared might be incredibly awful turned out to be quite superb. What is more, the copper exactly matched the red lacquer on the bed. The room was soon finished, and the atmosphere was totally different from that created by the Chinese symbols (page 40). The dove grey duchesse satin gave the illusion of mysterious grandeur and total luxury: the first night I felt like Marilyn Monroe swamped in all this satin.

The next morning I started to cut some more stencils for the bedspread and ornamental pillow covers. I cut a selection of flowers and buds with leaves, to be interspersed with the flying fish from the bathroom. These I stencilled on to the made-up counterpane: the flowers in the same gold used for the walls; the fish in copper. The pillow covers exactly fitted one of the wall stencils, so were quickly printed up. Satin has the most wonderful feeling, alas there was not enough for sheets and a duvet cover.

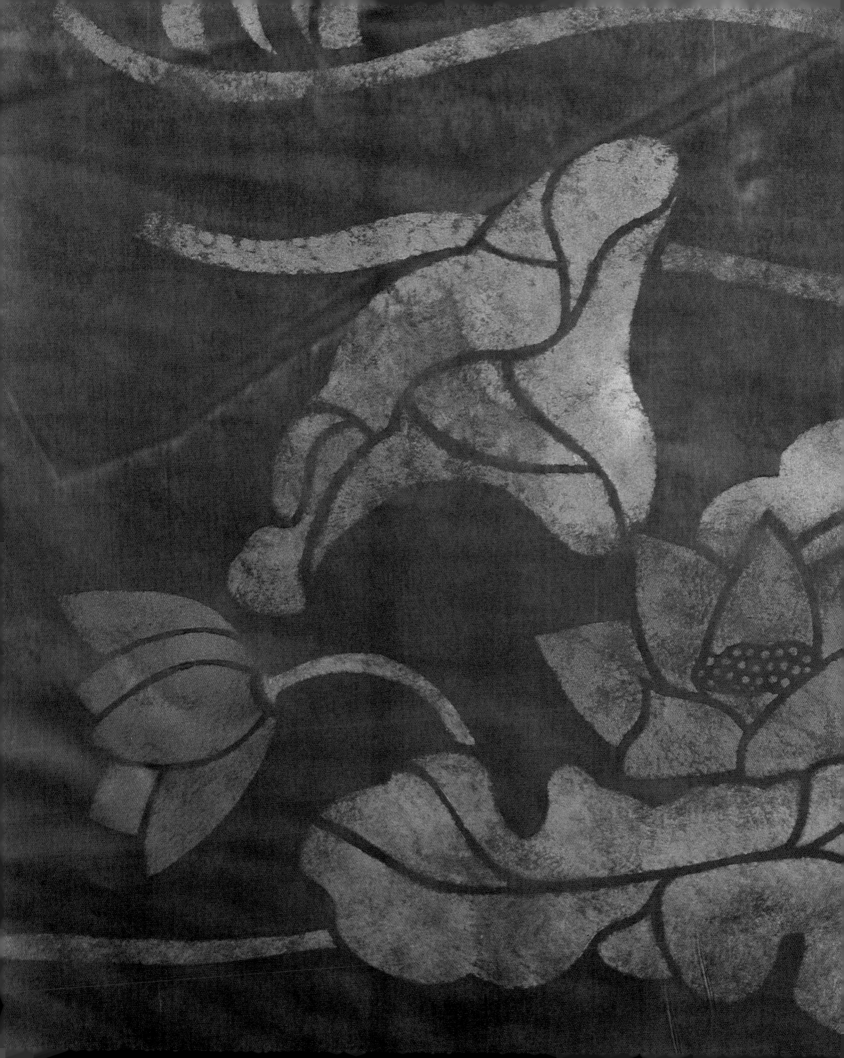

Rivers and Rushes

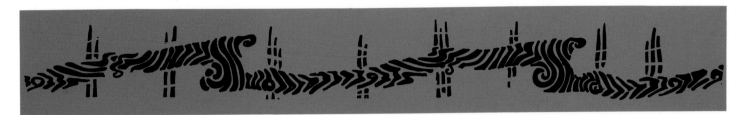

Once he had seen what could be done with cloth, my second brother asked to come with me to the East End next time I went to hunt for new fabrics. We made a bee-line for the section where I had found my satins. As I searched through the pile, James came across a roll of taffeta in what I can only describe as a true Victorian moss green (known then as reseda green). It was gorgeous. The roll was about 40m (45yds) long, and since it was cheap I bought him the whole length, thinking that I could use it if James changed his mind – which of course he did, saying that curtains made out of this luscious cloth would be too over the top for him.

The bathroom and bedroom were finished. All the furniture had now gone from the small spare room, including the Chinese bed, and all I had left in the store room were a black lacquered Queen Anne chest on stand and a pine Chinese Chippendale country edition lowboy (a side table with a drawer). I telephoned my mother and requisitioned a high-backed chair I had sold her, and this south-facing room now became a study. I decided that anybody who came to stay the night would have to sleep on the floor.

For once I came up with an idea which meant that I had to pattern-match on all four sides of the stencil. It seemed to take hours of kneeling on the floor and adjusting my pencilled lines to make it all match, but in the end it worked. On occasions when I begin to flag I remind myself that I only have to do this once, but that I might have to look at the design for years, so I had better pull myself together and do the thing properly from the start.

Triumph in Taffeta

This room was a real achievement for two reasons. Firstly the design was difficult because it had to be matched on all four sides of the stencil, and secondly when the cloth was printed and sewn together I was surprised at how well each drop aligned. I was also particularly pleased at the end to find I was left with enough material to make matching curtains.

The main theme was of swirling streams broken up by reeds. There were four sheets of design, each sheet being made up of two sheets of the large stencil paper. On the first length of cloth I used two sheets of the design repeated to the end of the length. On the second strip of material I used the third and fourth sheets of design, so that each alternative piece of cloth was different, but matched with the former piece. It sounds complicated but was not, and I was the most surprised at the perfect match I achieved.

The day I started to hang the cloth on the walls I was mystified when within ten minutes I found I was soaking wet. Since I did not feel ill and did not appear to have a temperature I ignored it and carried on working, nearly finishing two-thirds of the room by the evening. On listening to the news later I was amazed to hear that the temperature had reached over 32°c (90°F) during the day: as the room I was working in is half in the roof space it is no wonder I was almost overcome by heat.

The curtains were made from the same taffeta, and I printed the cloth in the same order as the walls so that the design would carry on. I self-lined them in the plain material, and then tried an experiment to ease draping using thin garden wire, which has turned out as planned (page 127). Once the curtains were hung and positioned I added the finishing touches: rosettes and some heavy bullion tassels I found in a box when hunting for curtain rings. When the sunlight shines through the curtains they appear almost to catch light as the gold is illuminated and the different shades in the satin are highlighted.

Acanthus Leaves

When buying the taffeta which eventually covered the walls of my small bedroom (page 115), I had picked up some sea-green duchesse satin. For the first time ever, green was in. I had grown up with the colour in every house I had lived in. Perhaps green velvet was cheap or something, but we certainly took advantage of it, and I swore that along with many other things I would never have green curtains or carpet. The latter has yet to come. My family always laughs, pointing out my habit of breaking solemn vows.

The Stairwell Curtains

I was lucky to find a hidden bale of green satin in a market which I immediately bought for the stairwell curtains. After I had machined two widths of cloth together I was ready to print my design, the only problem being that I could not quite decide what I wanted to do. While thumbing through a book on Tantric art, I noticed that a leaf design kept reappearing, which I realized closely resembled the western medieval acanthus leaf design. At first I found it difficult to draw, but once I had mastered the curves I drew up three different leaf clusters and a repeat border, which served for the edge of each curtain and the long swag.

When having tea with my brother Henry I chanced to pick up one of his books on Tantric art in India. The pictures contain the most amazing amount of detail, and I noticed that on a robe there was a design which was very similar to our medieval acanthus leaf motif. On closer study I became convinced that once again Europe had copied an idea from the Far East.

First I cut the border, which seemed to take an age as the pattern was really rather complicated, even in my poor copy, although it does not appear so. For some reason it did not flow for me. Once I had got the hang of the initial curves the small symbols were easier.

Although I have used this design for curtains I have a fancy that it might make a wonderful stole. When the curtains are taken down I intend to try it out. Although not lined, these curtains have wire inserted down the leading edges and also in the twists of cloth on the curtain swag (page 127). The advantage of this is that when you have pulled the cloth into position, instead of spending hours sewing the creases into place they just stay on command. This means that you can try several different effects without much effort at all.

Shades of Silver

This collection of cloth (right) has been stencilled using silver powders. The acanthus leaf design worked so well that I repeated it on panne velvet for a bed cover and bolster cushions. The Tibetan clouds in black overprinted in silver were intended as a blind, and the leopard and snake on grey melton make a throw which can be worn.

Fabric and Furnishing Techniques

Applying Cloth to Walls

The easiest method of applying material to walls is to employ an expert. On the other hand, if you are feeling adventurous and really want to try yourself, I will give you two alternatives to choose from. The first is the proper way, the second is mine.

Start off by battening the room, positioning the strips of wood at the top of the walls, as close to the ceiling as possible, and at floor level, then working your way up both sides of all corners and the chimney breast if there is one, and round the door frame and windows. Your next step is to staple bumph, or heavy duty interlining (already seamed), on to the battens, making sure that you cover the wood. Alternatively, you can staple up wadding, which does not need machining: just overlap it by about 2.5cm (1in). Whatever you choose as a lining, it must be pulled tight to make a good background for the top layer of cloth. One piece of advice which does help, is to do one wall at a time, otherwise you go mad, getting swamped in clouds of cloth. The next step is to put up the top layer of material, which must also be stretched very tight, but not so tight as to come away from the battens.

My way leaves most of this out. Firstly I cut the length of cloth required, plus 10cm (4in) in case odd things happen to the floor level, which they did in my house. Sew one wall of cloth together, mark the central points of both wall and material and get up a ladder. Matching up your points, place the cloth as close to the ceiling as possible and staple it into position on the wall, carrying on at 10-15cm (4-6in) intervals. Next staple each seam line to the skirting board, making sure that it hangs vertically and is pulled taut. Now go to the corners

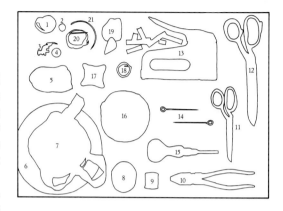

and, pulling the cloth as tight as you can without distorting the vertical seams, staple the material into position. Lastly, return to floor level, stretching the cloth without pulling it away from the top and stapling it into its final resting place.

EQUIPMENT
for textiles and furnishings
1 *Measuring tape*
2 *Thimble*
3 *Sewing machine zipper foot*
4 *Spool*
5 *Piping cord*
6 *Sewing box*
7 *Curtain heading tape*
8 *Thread*
9 *Thread*
10 *Pliers*
11 *Scissors*
12 *Dressmaker's scissors*
13 *Staple gun and staples*
14 *Upholstery skewers to hold cloth*
15 *Screwdriver*
16 *Black shoemaker's thread for upholstery*
17 *Pins on pin cushion*
18 *Plastic-covered garden wire*
19 *Tailor's chalk*
20 *Needle and thread*
21 *Upholsterer's curved needle*

Continue round the room in the same manner: any difficult areas where you cannot staple can either be glued or sewn with a curved needle.

Having joined all the lengths for the ceiling together, I was glad that I had left an extra 30cm (1ft) in length. This operation is rather like doing battle with a descending parachute. Most of the time I found it was a matter of guesswork. You have to spread the cloth out as best you can and attach with a staple gun on one side, matching the

EQUIPMENT
for applying cloth to walls
Staple gun and box of staples
Staple remover and tack lifter
Scissors
Measuring tape
Sewing machine and thread
Upholsterer's curved needle
Glue

seams up with the vertical seams on the wall. It is an idea to do the walls to either side next, stapling them at intervals to take the weight out of the material. These staples will have to be removed when you finally pull the cloth tight so try to use as few as possible. Matching up your vertical seams, pull the cloth as tight as you can and staple the second section of ceiling cloth into position. If the material is sagging in the middle of the ceiling you can always put some staples in the seam lines near the halfway mark. Then attack the side walls, pulling the cloth tight without letting the seam lines go astray. To give you courage, I found that I needed to allow two days for the whole operation. Don't stop, you haven't finished yet. Now you have to go round the room cutting off all excess cloth before gluing tape or ribbon down all the stapled edges.

Cushion Covers

After years of struggling I have only just learnt how to make cushion covers properly. Here is a guide which should make life easier for you.

Depending on the sort of cushion you prefer, tightly packed with stuffing or slightly looser, cut two squares of cloth for your intended cover up to 2.5cm (1in) smaller (for a firm cushion) or larger (for a softer one) than the pad plus a seam allowance. Stencil your chosen motif on to the cloth squares. While this is drying start to prepare your welting. This is made from piping cord covered with cloth cut on the bias, which is then sewn round the cushion to make an edging. Whatever the size of welting you choose, the cloth must be cut to allow a 1.25cm (½in) seam allowance to either side.

To make up the welting, start by measuring the perimeter of the cushion, adding about 5cm (2in) extra, then cut out strips of cloth going across the grain on the bias. This allows the cloth to stretch evenly round the corner without going lumpy or creasing. Usually you need to make several seams in the casing, and these should be sewn on the

straight of the weave (that is on the diagonal of the strips of cloth). It helps, when you have cut the strips, to trim the tops and bottoms on the same weave so that the seams will all lie in the same direction. Lay one of your strips on the work surface, pattern side up, and do the same with the second strip, bringing the cut edges together. Holding the right-hand strip and keeping the raw edges together, turn it on to its wrong side, where it should lie at right angles to the other. Line the whole thing up and machine with a tight stitch, then press flat. Lay your piping cord on to the wrong side of the material strip, and either tack it into place or, using the zipper foot with the stitch length set on medium to small, machine the casing together, keeping the material pulled as tightly round the cord as you can. The zipper foot enables you to stitch very close to the cord.

Place one of the printed squares, which should now be dry, on to the work surface with the design uppermost. Chalk up the seam line and place the welting with the seam allowance facing towards the edge of the square, matching the machine stitching with the chalk. Tack it into place. To avoid 'ears' on the finished cushion lead the welting round each corner in a curve, not at right angles. If the material covering the piping cord is pulling, just snip to the machine line every 0.5cm (¼in) which will allow the welting free movement round the corners.

To join the welting, cut off any excess cloth and cord to within 2.5cm (1in), trimming back the cord to form a butt join. Do not cut the casing off, but bend in the raw edge to cover the butt join and tack it into place. Using the zipper foot, attach the welting with a tight stitch. Finally add the second half of your cover, wrong side up, and machine into position, sewing 5cm (2in) past each corner of the last side leaving enough space to slide the cushion pad into the cover. Cut the seam allowance diagonally across each corner to reduce the bulk of the cloth, then turn the cushion inside out. Insert the cushion pad, then hand-sew the opening closed.

EQUIPMENT
for making cushion covers
Measuring tape and ruler
Scissors
Tailor's chalk or soft pencil
Piping cord
Dressmaker's pins
Sewing machine and thread

EQUIPMENT
for making table-cloths
Measuring tape
Scissors
String
Tailor's chalk or soft pencil
Dressmaker's pins
Sewing machine and thread

Leopard Cloth

Dark purple glazed chintz was chosen for this circular cloth to set off the wine red damask of the chair. Gold powders in two shades were used to stencil the leopard and snake design, adding a dramatic touch to a pale room.

Table-cloths

Another decorative item which I have always said I hated and would never use is the round table-cloth. I could hardly believe what I was hearing when I suggested to someone that I could make and print up a pair of cloths for them: I really should stop making statements of any kind, as it would appear that I am always changing my opinions.

Drape a tape measure over the centre of the table top, letting it hang to the floor on each side. Cut lengths of cloth a few centimetres (inches) longer than this, joining up the widths until you have a square of cloth. Iron down the seams, then fold the cloth into quarters and lay it flat on a work surface. Halve your original measurement, add 5cm (2in) for the hem and cut a piece of string to this length. Attach a piece of chalk to one end, and place the other on the corner of your square. Draw an arc on the material with the chalk, then carefully cut round this line through the four thicknesses of material. You should have a perfect circle.

You can line the cloth by repeating the whole procedure, then matching the wrong sides of the two circles together and sewing them, leaving space to turn the cloth right-side out. Trim and snip the hem, then reverse the cloth and press the seams flat. If you are not using a lining, go round the cloth with chalk and a piece of card marked with the hem allowance chalking the hem line every 7-10cm (3-4in). With a hot iron press up the hem, then stitch the cloth into place.

The same basic process can be used for oblong table-cloths. Round corners are more practical than square ones, which trail all over the floor and in my experience always get sucked up by the vacuum cleaner. I achieved the best results by putting the cloth on the table and marking with a pin each of the table's corners in turn. Measure the distance from the table top to the floor plus hem allowance with string, and attach a piece of chalk to one end of the string. Lift the corner of the cloth on to the table and, holding the string on the pinned corner, draw your curve and

then cut it out. Follow with the other corners, then finish sewing the hem all round. There may be other ways of doing this, but for me this seems the most accurate method.

As with the curtains, all this is done before you print up your stencilled pattern. If you want to cut a border stencil, use the finished edge of the cloth as a guide to the shape you need.

Curtains and Blinds

I always make up curtains and blinds before I stencil them so that I can be sure that the design is correctly positioned on the fabric. Do not gather them until you have finished the stencilling because the fabric must be as flat and unwrinkled as possible. The

Tiger Hall

I treated the dress curtains in my hallway in the most exotic fashion I could think of. Because the front door is so high I tried to unify the room by hanging the curtains at the same level, which also makes the room look grander by keeping the 2.4m (8ft) table in proportion. The carving over the door focuses the eye so that you look outside at the small courtyard.

type of curtain or blind you choose will depend on where you want to use them, but I have worked out a number of very easy methods of making them look sumptuous, which you might find useful.

SWAGGING

I first decided to try my hand at swagging when I thought I had finished decorating the Portuguese drawing room (page 34). Somehow the atmosphere of the room was too austere, and slowly it dawned on me that the straight line made by the top of the blinds needed softening. So I dug out some cloth left over from the blinds and some antique tassels and decided to have a go.

First of all I pinned up the silk tassel cording in large loops. Then, taking strips of cloth 60cm (2ft) wide and

to ask the easiest way of making them, and she kindly instructed me over the phone. Having always wondered how they were made I will pass on the recipe.

Using a round tray – I chose one which measured about 49cm (19in) in circumference – lay it on the cloth and draw round it with a pencil. Cut this circle out and use it as a template for the other rosettes. Next sew 2.5cm (1in) long running stitches round the perimeter of the circle, about 2cm (¾in) in from the edge. Gather the cloth together and stitch it, securing the thread. You will now have a bag: fluff it out, then flatten it like a pancake. Push the needle through the neck of the bag, coming up in the middle of the flattened cloth. Start scrunching the cloth into rose-like folds (at this stage it looks rather like a brain) and start sewing them into place, working your way from the middle to the outside.

At first the whole thing looks like a complete mess, but keep going: the end result is quite unbelievable. Unfortunately you do not have much time to admire your handiwork as you still have the rest to do (another *eleven* in my case for the Portuguese drawing room). Finally you can position them on the swag and sew them into place. By adjusting the folds, I have since made three different kinds of rosette, some more like full-blown rose blooms, others really tight.

Portuguese Swag

This swag was part of the Portuguese room decoration (page 34). For the main window I had a pair of antique tassels, but for this one I had to improvise and dye a new cord to match the looped tie-back. White drill was swagged over the supporting tie-back and sewn into place so that the whole creation would not collapse when the blind was let down. Rosettes served two purposes, they looked more opulent and hid the raw cloth ends.

about twice the width of the window in length, I started with the middle of the cloth at the middle of the blind, and threaded the material through the loops, forming a swag as I went, by pinning and pushing the cloth into soft drapes and curves.

Having pinned up one half of the swag I found it impossible to match the other half without getting down from the ladder every two minutes. At this rate I would never finish. So I invited one of my brothers round, provided him with tea and biscuits and positioned him in a chair from which he could give directions while I went up the ladder. The operation was soon completed. Having assured myself that the swags were sumptuous enough, I then set about hand-sewing them to the blind, so that the whole effect would not collapse when the blind was lifted or dropped.

ROSETTES

Once the swags were done in the Portuguese drawing room, rosettes were the last task. I telephoned a friend

RUCHED PELMETS

Another successful way of making windows more sumptuous is to add ruched pelmets. I did this in the drawing room once it had been hung with water-marbled paper (page 20).

Taking lengths of calico which had come off another window, I laboriously painted them black with the same emulsion as used on the blinds. Not only did this ensure a perfect colour match, but it also made the cloth stiff as cardboard, an unexpected bonus of which I took full advantage. When it was dry I stencilled it using two or three shades of gold powders with the Persian ribbon design.

I attached the ruched cloth to the large blind in three separate sections, each pleated and stapled to the top of the blind. Then I positioned the silk tassels to hold the cloth in place. Because the painted calico was so stiff I found it almost impossible to sew, and the only way to form the ruches was actually to push it into place, where it seemed to stay. Obviously where the cloth was bent into shape it must have cracked the paint surface, although this does not show.

WIRING

This technique was the result of a successful experiment in the study (page 115). Normally I hand-sew curtain linings into place, but this time I machined the material together, turned the curtain to the right side, ironed all the seams and the leading edge, and pinned green plastic-covered thin garden wire all the way down and along the bottom of the curtain. I then machined it into place as tightly as possible, using the zipper foot as for welting a cushion. Once the wire was held in place I found that I could twist and turn the cloth to any shape that took my fancy. This technique can also be used on unlined curtains.

Avoiding Upholstery

If you cannot afford to have your chairs re-upholstered each time you want to change the cloth covers, and do not have the time or inclination to try doing it yourself, I have discovered a quick way of overcoming the problem, which I used when I was doing my Persian Ribbons and Carnations design.

Lay your printed length of cloth over the chair, then push the material into position as though it were a loose cover. Secure and tidy any loose pieces of material either with pins or by sewing with a curved needle. This is the treatment I have given the black and green chair in the drawing room. It seems to be satisfactory, and nobody has stuck themselves with the pins yet.

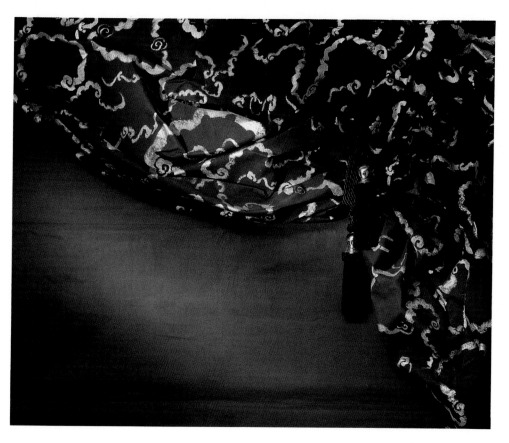

Persian Swag

This is the same window and blind as opposite but painted with black emulsion (page 93). In order to ensure an exact colour match I laboriously painted the swag and stencilled the Persion ribbons in a variety of gold shades. The cloth was pleated at the top and stapled to the blind heading. The material had become so stiff that I could not sew the swag into position and had to rely on the black-and-brass tie-back to hold it in place.

I discovered another solution when doing the Fighting Tigers room (page 84). I had been given a broken-down Victorian copy of a seventeenth-century chair by an old friend who was a dealer. It was originally to have gone to my brother, but when he was offered this free bundle of sticks I detected a curling of the lip, so kept the chair in store for myself. Now I wanted to effect an immediate cure. One arm was missing so I threw the survivor out. The seat needed re-upholstering with webbing, horsehair and the rest, all of which was in store, so I asked a carpenter to sort out an offcut of plywood and slap it over the hole. This done, out came the filler and paintbrush. While waiting for the paint to dry, I printed up a piece of yellow cloth with persian carnations in black and gold. This I stapled to the chair seat to form a decorative undercover for the cushion which had already been made for the top. This took only a couple of hours, cost practically nothing, and has the most original end result which is comfortable as well as looking different.

Index